W.H. AUDEN

The Commissar and the Yogi
W.H. AUDEN
A Study of His Plays and Longer Poems

M. Kumaraswamy Raju

PRESTIGE

Published by
Prestige Books
3/28, East Patel Nagar, New Delhi 110 008
in association with
Indian Society for Commonwealth Studies
New Delhi

ISBN: 81-85218-25-0

Jacket design by
3-A Corporation,
New Delhi 110 002

Phototypesetting by
data culture
New Delhi 110 065
Ph. 6431070

Printed at
Mehra Offset Press
New Delhi 110 002

Contents

Acknowledgments

I owe an irredeemable debt of gratitude to Bhagawan Sri Sathya Sai Baba for blessing my every endeavour; Prof. M.V. Rama Sarma M.A., Ph.D (Wales), formerly Vice-Chancellor, Sri Venkateswara University, Tirupati for guiding me in this study on W.H. Auden; Padmabhusan Prof. C.D. Narasimhaiah for his loving and affectionate care; William B. Hunter, Texas, U.S.A., who considered my research a "superior work" and found it publishable by "our own (U.S.A.) presses"; Prof. C. Subba Rao and Prof. K. Venkatachari, Andhra Pradesh Open University, Hyderabad for their valuable insights; Prof. K. Venkata Reddy, Vice-Chancellor, Sri Krishnadevaraya University, Anantapur for the encouragement to publish this book; the A.S.R.C., Hyderabad for providing me with critical material; the U.G.C. for providing partial financial assistance to publish this book; Dr. R.K. Dhawan, University of Delhi, for his memorable advice in finding a publisher, and M/S Prestige Books for bringing out this book elegantly.

M. KUMARASWAMY RAJU

Lord, teach me to write so well, that I shall no longer want to.

W.H. Auden

Preface

That Auden is one of the significant poets of the present century, few would dispute. A prolific poet of extraordinary virtuosity, Auden's creative career spans virtually four significant decades of 20th century history. His poetic genius appears to be at once a blessing and a curse in a special sense. Very few twentieth century poets could boast of such range and depth, variety and strength, relevance and authenticity. His lightness of touch which is never light-hearted, much less "light," is something the critics found difficult to adequately appreciate. His virtuosity and tireless quest for the right form, and his bravura—all have been used against him. Far from being considered as marks of excellence these have been regarded as slick and slight, wholly lacking in seriousness. He has frequently been type-cast into the English Auden and the American Auden, the Commissar and the Yogi, in search of a God that would never fail him, and a prodigy who betrayed himself and his friends around 1940.

In the face of such response and reaction to a basically complex poet, whose irony spares nothing including the mode of irony, stylistic roots reach deep and far into the Anglo-Saxon and the Icelandic sagas, there is a need, in the first place, to sift the dramatic from the lyrical, the serious from the comic, the ephemeral from the universal in his work. Although neat pigeonholing is suspect, a working classification would clarify and put into focus the central concerns of Auden. In other words, the implicit assumption here is that one can detect a seamless, unbroken continuity in Auden's basic preoccupation with life. In fact, the early and the later Auden, the English and the American, the Leftist and the religious—divisions that we all too easily tend to take for granted—prevent us from getting at the real Auden, the "authentic" in his work, as he himself puts it. What is claimed here is that a latent strain could be seen lurking in his several preoccupations, in the evolving concerns of the poet, constituting a daring creative experiment in 20th century image-making, at once reflecting the shared experience of modern life in a uniquely personal idiom. It would, therefore, be less than just to demarcate Auden's work into neat little compartments. While each of the phases has its relevance and meaning, it would be proper to regard them as catalysts at a crucial stage in the evolution of the poet.

Right from the beginning, Auden acted as a sensitive register reflecting a variety of ideologies, and items absorbing them into the structure of the work. No wonder he is styled as 'the sage of anxiety,' a felicitous phrase which he would himself have loved. His chief concern is man in relation to himself, in relation to society and in relation to the Supreme Being. Auden's early admiration for Hardy's hawk's vision, his way of looking at life from a very great height enabled him to see the individual life related not only to the local social life of its time, but to the whole of human history.

The present study seeks, in a modest way, to analyze the implications of the supposed or real betrayal of the Marxist cause in favour of Kierkegaardian Christianity and examine the problematic nature of the continuity between the works of the thirties and of the forties. In Chapter I, an attempt has been made to trace the evolution of the poet in relation to his works. An account of the impact of the psychologists Freud, Jung, Groddeck, Homer Lane, the dialectics of Marx and Engels, the dramaturgic concepts of the German playwright Brecht, the influence of Neibuhr and Kierkegaard on Auden is given. It is shown how Auden's German trip becomes crucial in shaping the form and content of his plays and how lasting this impact is. Although one likes to demarcate Auden's evolution into such phases as the Freudian phase, the Marxist phase or the Kierkegaardian phase, in the ultimate analysis, these categorizations disappear and one sees a continuing and developing engagement with the predicament of modern man in Auden's plays and longer poems. Whether it is the plays of the thirties or the longer poems of the forties, Auden's interest lay in man in society. Each of the subsequent chapters discusses Auden's major works of the thirties and the forties, primarily in terms of theme, and how it informs their form.

The large volume of work turned out during 1928-1973 with a wide array of metrical forms, rhyme-schemes and structural patterns suggesting each kind of form needed a different sort of modality or a tone, Auden's work eludes the focus the researcher desperately seeks. Since Auden's plays have not received the critical attention they deserve and since the longer poems have often been dismissed as "doddering shadows" of his earlier work, it has been thought convenient to focus on them and to show the constancy of his major themes. It is not an exaggeration to suggest that the test of the true worth of a poet lies in success or defeat in attempting a long poem. At least from the time of the Romantics, this has become a special criterion which measures the greatness of a poet. And from this point of view, Auden undergoes a very successful trial in the accomplished productions of his longer poems and plays. What appears to be a hopeless ordeal unsuccessfully gone through by other contemporary poets in the hands of Auden becomes an energetic display of power, mastery and meaning. Both from the point of view of structure and texture, Auden overcomes the inevitable hurdles encountered by a poet in the composition of a long poem. Hence the choice of longer poems for this study. Auden's success in the short poem has been established but here an attempt is made to show the energy and power of the verse essay. Chapters 2 to 8 offer a reading of the individual plays and the longer poems—followed by the conclusion.

The Commissar and the Yogi
The Paradoxical Nature of W.H. Auden's Imagination

An outstanding innovator, experimentalist and ironist, W.H. Auden (1907-1973) may be said to have given a new life to time-worn forms of English verse not by any break with convention but by "daring and original levies on tradition."[1] It is astonishing that not until the last years of his life did his inventiveness decline as evidenced by his style becoming gossipy and diction tending towards "linguistic rarities." Rarely in modern times has any other poet experimented with such a wide variety of forms of poetry as the ballad, the ode, the elegy, the verse play, the opera libretti, the sonnet sequence, the verse meditation, not to speak of occasional poems, sestinas, limericks and other kinds of light verse in such a manner as to fit them to modern conditions and occasions. His was a presence forceful enough to fuel a revolution in the Thirties—a revolution in "form and content" which was to set the course for English poetry for decades to come. However, at a time which witnessed daring experimentation and even deconstruction of poetic form, Auden stood for rules in poetry which stemmed from his belief that no poetic form was indeed beyond resurrection or resuscitation. Indeed, he has shown a mastery of not only the traditional accentual syllabic metres of Anglo-American origin but also of French syllabic metres besides the Anglo-Saxon alliterative verse which points to an astounding virtuosity seldom encountered during the past two hundred years. His poetry bears the impress of the most significant intellectual currents of his time although in the present age of disbelief he seemed to have turned 'reactionary' with his pronounced Anglicanism after having been a Leftist. But his Christian faith is derived from existential theology rather than orthodox doctrine unlike Eliot's which sprang from the sermons of Lancelot Andrews. As a critic he stands comparison with Eliot, Pound, Tate, Ransom and even Lionel Trilling who have all promoted an awareness of contemporary sensibility through their creative and critical works. It is undeniable that his verse is educative and entertaining irrespective of the form in which it is cast or come to assume just as his criticism will be found significant because of its brilliant exposition of the poet's confrontation with himself and his world.

The intellectualist critical establishment between the Wars in the present century under the tutelege of T.S. Eliot made poetry problematic by virtue of its uncompromising anti-romantic stance and dialectical method reminiscent of the Metaphysicals at their best. This is further complexified by the poet's awareness of the widening gap between faith and reason, the power of science and moral comprehension which has changed the world out of all recognition and sealed all escapes from self and its menacing environment. The poets have found it alarming that human choices have become severely restricted and that man seems trapped in "a monolithic technical world" which being capable of even imposing its own methods upon dissent, has to be transcended in the interests of freedom and survival. Concomitant with this is the rise of a kind of neo-orthodoxy which actually spelt a 'crisis-theology' occasioned by the currency of existentialism, Marxism, socialist realism, secular modernism and even Fundamentalism. Surprisingly, Auden's own faith came to be influenced by these new currents of thought in such a way as to reinforce it rather than dissolve it which explains his life-long preoccupation with concerns essentially Christian rather than secular.

It is significant that the most distinguished poets of the present time including Auden have been poet-critics who view criticism as a corollary to creation. It is an awareness of the larger contexts in which the poem is born and bred which has led to an insistence on the autonomy of the poem, a poetic universe which is subject to its own laws. I.A. Richards's *Principles of Literary Criticism* (1929) affords the lesson "that we should not criticise the poem but it is the poem that criticises us" as pointed out by Lawrence Lipking.[2] The emergence of so-called New Criticism is but the outcome of thinking that has sought to establish the primacy of the poem and its self-sufficiency. The critical monism which the New Critical strategies have given rise to have had its impact on the poetry of Auden, which may be regarded as 'poetry of inclusion' although it does not share any of the important traits of the poetry of Ransom, Tate, Randall Jarrell and Wallace Stevens. This is but to be expected because of Auden's own interest in revivifying poetic forms and strategies which do not seem to have found favour with the aforesaid poets.

Derided as a 'chameleon poet' for whom the dogmas of one year are likely to become heresies in the following year, Auden has had to contend with a criticism which is singularly inappreciative of his developing phylogenetic vision. It is argued that the writing of such diverse works as *The Dance of Death* and *For the Time Being* constitutes a breach of faith just as his emigration to the U.S. from his native country on the eve of the World War II is tantamount to a breach of loyalty. Without going into his possible motives for 'deserting' his native land in its hour of travail, it is possible to regard it as pacificist act having no meaning beyond itself although it cannot be asserted in the absence of any irrefutable evidence. However, it may be suggested that the seeming transition from the vision embodied in *The Dance of Death* to that of *For the Time Being* is not a transition from a secularization of the spiritual to the spiritualization of the secular but different expressions of an imagination that is intellectualist rather than emotional in character. Stephen Spender saw in him "a man who, instead of Being . . . romantically confused, diagnosed the contemporary society, and of civilization . . . with our neuroses. He found symptoms everywhere."[3] Auden's distinction lies in transmuting symptoms into rich imagery instinct with experiential and existential implications which is the reason why his poetry may be said to distil as it were the whole of Western philosophy as has come to influence the Western World of modern times. However, any attempt to categorize his work as Marxian, Freudian, existentialist will deny it its unified vision and significance.

An important aspect of Auden's poetry of the Thirties is its diagnostic interest. His wide reading in psycho-analysis helped him to diagnose the diseases of not only his friends but of others as well. As a poet of 'angst' he tried to analyze the human self from different perspectives. For him, "The basic human problem is man's anxiety in time e.g., his present anxiety over himself in relation to his past and his parents (Freud), his present anxiety over himself in relation to his future and his neighbours (Marx), his present anxiety over himself in relation to eternity and God ((Kierkegaard)."[4]

W.H. Auden is primarily the spokesman of the Thirties and in any discussion of them his name comes up prominently in bold relief: "the mention of Auden almost automatically conjures up visions of the Thirties. To a lesser extent, the converse is also true: in any discussion of the Thirties the name of Auden is likely to be one of the first to crop up. As far as poetry goes the two are nearly synonymous."[5] This is no mean achievement considering that W.B. Yeats, T.S. Eliot, David Jones and Dylan Thomas were the leading poets of that time. He seemed to be the one poet in whom "the phenomena of the age" were "mirrored in anything like their daily habit and diversity."[6]

The Nineteen Thirties, the decade described by Auden in his poem "September I, 1939"[7] as "a low dishonest decade," was the period in which young writers were involved in the politics of the Left. The Leftist bias of English poetry was noticeable in the writings of Osbert Sitwell, Siegfreid Sassoon, Robert Graves and Wilfred Owen even as early as 1918. A few writers voiced their revolutionary ideas through *The Daily Herald,* a newspaper, and *The New Statesman* and *The Nation*, the weeklies, all of which were Leftist. There was no orthodoxy of the Right among the writers of the older generation corresponding to that of the intellectual Left. The scene in the third decade was fast changing, thanks to changes in socio-economic and political conditions. Many assumptions previously taken for granted in middleclass democratic Europe were proved wrong by the growing unemployment among workers, hunger marches, dole queues, street fighting between Fascists and Communists and such other events which were witnessed in the Thirties. Some of the consequences of the First World War were terrible. Auden describes "Depressed Areas," "Smokeless Chimneys, damaged bridges, rotting wharves and choked canals." The climactic event of the decade was Hitler's assumption of German Chancellorship which eventually led to the outbreak of World War in September 1939. The picture that emerges from this is not essentially different from that projected by T.S. Eliot's *The Waste Land*—a picture that delineates in purely physical terms what *The Waste Land* does in psychosomatic terms namely the catastrophic consequences of the war that shook the Western World to its foundations. Such a bleak view of the world lying in social and spiritual ruins is expressive of the traumatic experience that the war spelt for Auden and Eliot, although it induced different reactions in them. While T.S. Eliot turned towards religion, Auden, at least initially, sought solutions in Marxist ideology which explained in terms of dialectical materialism what seemed to have gone wrong with the world. Such a development was not unexpected because it was during the Thirties that marked by the loss of faith that the intellectuals came under the spell of what might be termed the Messianic message of Karl Marx. But as future events had shown it was for intellectuals like Auden only a brief "encounter" before the disenchantment with the dream ensued. This however should not be regarded as any comment on Marxist ideology as such but a description of a fact that concerned several other leading intellectuals of Europe including Auden, Andre Gide, Arthur Koestler, to mention the most outstanding among them.

Julian Symons's *The Thirties: A Dream Revolved* (1960), William H. Pritchard's *Seeing Through Everything* (1977), George Watson's *Politics and Literature in Modern Britain* (1977), Stephen Spender's *The Thirties and After* (1978), and Bernard Bergonzi's *Reading the Thirties* (1978)[8] all deal with politics and literature of the 1930s. Donald Davie's poem "Remembering the Thirties" memorializes the Auden generation and it is a brilliant evocation of a "fabulous" decade. Christopher Isherwood's *Lions and Shadows* (1938) and Stephen Spender's *World Within World* (1951) are autobiographical works with special emphasis on the private world of Auden and his group. Isherwood's fictional autobiography brings out the "Mortmere" myth fashioned by the group, its jokes, its fantasies, its preferences and prejudices.[9] For

Julian Symons, *Lions and Shadows* is "lively, subtle, fresh, but . . . offers no more than an illusion of frankness."[10] Spender's book deals with Auden group in general focussing in particular on his intimate relationship with Auden.

Literary historians have often described the Thirties as a literary movement with Auden as its leader. Called 'MacSpaunday' the movement was identified with C. Day Lewis, Auden, MacNeice and Stephen Spender. They were also collectively called "the Gang," "the Auden Group" or "the Leftist Poets," all pejorative terms, the only warm reference made by Donald Davie being "the Veterans." Although it was common practice to bracket Auden, Day Lewis, MacNeice and Spender together and label them as one wished, recent criticism questioned the validity of it. This conforms to what the poets themselves came to think of it. While Auden dismissed the linkage as absurd, Day Lewis remarked, "we did not know we were a movement until the critics told us we were."[11] Spender was no less vehement in denying the grouping made by critics: "Movements have meetings, issue manifestoes, have aims in common. The Thirties' poets never held a single meeting, they issued no manifestoes. . . . They wrote very different kinds of poetry without anyone of them feeling that, in doing so, he was letting down the side. As I have mentioned elsewhere, the first time that Auden, Day Lewis and Spender were all three in a room together was in Venice, after the war, in 1948."[12]

Pronouncements apart, clear evidence is provided by *Oxford Poetry* volumes (1925 to 1930) as regards the divergence and variety of themes and attitudes marking their poetry. Significantly, although Auden, Day Lewis, MacNeice, Rex Warner had all published their poems in *Oxford Poetry,* only Spender's poem, "Now You've no work, like a rich man. . .", had a political theme. Moreover, Day Lewis's *Beechen Vigil* (1925), *Country Comets* (1928), *Transitional Poem* (1929), MacNeice's *Blind Fireworks* (1929), Auden's *Poems* (1928) were not predicated on political issues. Of Spender's *Nine Experiments* (1928) and *Twenty Poems* (1930), only *Written Whilst Walking Down the Rhine* could be said to be concerned with a political theme. It should be obvious that as Spender himself clarified, he was the only one who was "always interested in politics'' while Auden's interests ''were poetry, psychoanalysis and medicine.''[13]

Rather than saying that there was a literary movement with a plan and an action programme, it would be true to say that it was Auden who exercised a marked influence on his contemporaries. Spender describes Auden at Oxford as one who ''was didactic, dogmatic even, but in no way dictatorial. He gave no orders. He was a consciousness and he heightened consciousness in others but he did not demand that they should imitate him. He was extravagant in all he said, and in his behaviour. His way was the way of excess and this, though it led to the palace of wisdom, does not demand obedience. Moreover, he was extremely funny, overacting the role of Auden and saying things in a way which caricatured them even as he did so. He had nothing about him of the pure intellectual who talks about values and recognizes none but his own.''[14] The foregoing testifies to Auden's power over his friends and explains his dominance.

At Oxford, his wit and intellectual force rendered him a central figure. His earliest poetic model was Thomas Hardy who was followed by Edward Thomas, Wilfred Owen, A.E. Housman, Edwin Arlington Robinson, Robert Frost, Robert Graves and Laura Riding. The publication of Eliot's *The Waste Land* (1922) brought about a ''palace revolution'' and changed Auden's thinking about poetry. About this time he became aware of the work of Gerald Manley Hopkins and came to formulate theories of poetry. For example, he told Spender that ''the subject of a poem is only a peg on which to hang the poetry.''[15] A poet was a kind of chemist who mixed his poems out of words, whilst remaining detached from his own feelings. Feelings and emotional experiences were only the occasion which precipitated into his mind the idea of a poem. Eliot's theories of impersonality and his objective correlative are constantly echoed in Auden's Oxford pronouncements. His clinical detachment is allied to Eliot's practice.

After leaving Oxford, Auden went to Germany as he was drawn towards German Literature and German Culture. Although most Englishmen were going to France to glimpse ''the lost generation,'' Auden, partly influenced by his interest in Germanic sagas and old English poetry, which he had discovered through the Oxford lectures of J.R.R.. Tolkien, chose to visit Germany. The effect of his stay there on his poetry, plays and his thinking was considerable. That writers like Rilke, Brecht, Kafka, Freud and Marx, German popular songs, the work of Kierkegaard, and the whole German Protestant tradition formed and shaped his writing was beyond doubt.

The influence of Bertolt Brecht on the political attitudes embodied in the early poetry and the plays of Auden appears to be considerable. Auden himself admits to a change in his thinking after his German trip. He "knew no German and no German literature" at first but made great progress soon after. He confronted a climate of thought and feeling upon which he would draw as he began to write political verse at a time when England itself was developing a climate analogous to that of Germany. Here, under the influence of John Layard who supplemented and complemented Homer Lane, Freud, Groddeck, Auden continued using a partially comic and fantastic analysis to diagnose sicknesses. Also, Berlin was a crucial factor in Auden's development in that the connection between art and politics in Germany during the Weimar years was so close that there was scarcely any artistic document that could not be seen within a political context. Literature and politics were interlinked. Frederick Buell points out a remarkable correspondence between Auden's early themes and certain aspects of Weimar politics and culture: "In Berlin, Auden encountered, in a new and dramatic form, many of the preoccupations, worries, and interests of his generation in England; as is always the case with Auden, whether travelling in Berlin or Iceland, or reading Freud, Marx or Kierkegaard, one senses that he has gone there only to meet something of himself."[16]

Though Auden scholars have isolated Brecht as an important literary source underlying Auden's political and dramaturgic ideas, critics like Breon Mitchell strongly opposed it:

> As for Brecht, Auden was certainly influenced to some degree by the *Dreigroschenoper* and *Mahagonny*, the first of which

> he saw while in Berlin (1928), but, we must remember, at a time when he was only beginning to learn German, he was also familiar with some of the songs from *Mahagonny* which had been printed at this time in the *Hauspostille* collection. The play itself was not produced in Berlin until 21 December, 1931. Auden feels the influence upon his plays to have been slight at best, and certainly not of major importance (This is not to deny a more profound influence upon his poetry. He had read and enjoyed Brecht's *Hauspostille* Poems (1927), as mentioned above, but feels this did not influence his plays. He still prefers Brecht's lyric poetry to the dramatic works.[17]

Mitchell's persuasive argument against making much out of a relatively limited literary contact finds strong support in the discovery of such other influences as Cocteau, Ibsen and the English Christmas pantomime.

The reasons for relating Auden to Brecht are not far to seek. Both being Left wingers have sought a literary mode of articulation for their polemic—a mode that predictably was predicated on the technique of satire. Their final aim seems to be the creation of a living vision of reality broad enough to enclose the rational and the irrational, the real and the unreal—a reality the source of which is the imagination. Their purpose seems to be to view unreason from the point of view of reason which comes close to Kafka's concept of irrationality. Such a procedure is justifiable in that even modern science in order to probe the nature of reality situates the object of investigation in experimental, that is, artificial conditions. This is what imparts to much of their work the quality of psychological naturalism which is rendered all the more potent through their use of realistic symbolism. Even the tone of mock-seriousness characterizing their work is traceable to their interest in the realization of estrangement (Verfremdungs effect)—a non-involvement in the aesthetic experience afforded by the work of art—in order that judgment might be possible which points to their exalted view of art and its power. The use of the dream in Auden's works may be considered as an attempt to see the ultimate reality in terms of what might be termed limited reality represented often by the waking state although it does not create a nightmare-world as it does in the works of Ionesco. The anguish in Auden's plays is traceable to his viewing man as a symbol of a conflict between his fears largely subconscious and his hopes of his redeeming himself and his world.

Just as Brecht carried on experiments in form and matter, Auden too attempted to cultivate novelty in form and content. In *Paid on Both Sides* (1928), *The Orators* (1932), *The Dance of Death* (1933), *The Dog Beneath the Skin* (1935), *The Ascent of F6* (1936), *On the Frontier* (1938) and *Letter from Iceland* (1937), Auden "attempted an experiment with both the mixing of different genres and juxtaposition of different kinds of content, and one of the principal reasons for the sense of freedom, of poetic liberation, that his work gave his contemporaries that just this use of 'connections on everyside'."[11] Brecht wanted to absorb elements of popular culture into art and tried to turn a great many popular genres into literary or quasi-literary ones but he also drew upon popular culture for much of the substance of certain of his dramas. But, while Brecht took care to sustain his epic theatre, Auden did not flinch from rendering experience in an episodic, incidental and sketch-like manner.

The Dance of Death (1933), written at the time of Hitler's assumption of power, is an example of Auden's conscious attempts to come to grips with German materials and to integrate them into the English political scene. Its theme of "death-wish" and its setting are transplanted into England. Germany is superimposed on England so that the capitalist crisis, as Marx put it, is not a local but a global phenomenon. *The Dance of Death* like *Mahagonny* is written for entertainment but, at the same time, it attacks the idea of entertainment and the society that fosters it. The Marxist thesis, indeed, proves helpful for tying up his thematic threads at the focal points of the play and Marx himself appears on the stage to lend credence to it.

Returning home from Germany, Auden published *Poems* (1930) which included *Paid on Both Sides, The Orators* (1932) and *The Dance of Death* (1933). Auden's analysis of society based on his reading in Freud, Lawrence and a host of psychological writers was at the centre of *Paid on Both Sides*. The allegorical landscape of Auden's poetry before 1933 consisted of a sick society, a society in which individuals repressed their instinctive, spontaneous impulses. With their instincts freed, individuals would become healthy and society would be cured. *The Orators* is the best illustration of Auden's diagnostic poetry. *Paid on Both Sides* is concerned with hereditary feuds projecting an alarming vision of the English bourgeoisie class facing its gravest crisis of history. Coming as it did soon after Auden's return from Germany, this early play could be attributed to a belief in the Marxist apocalypse and the Germanism of the poet's sensibility.

The Dance of Death is also partly based on Auden's psychological theme. The dancer in the play represents sickness or death-wish of society whose health depends not so much on society's health as on its sickness. The dancer is shown passing through two episodes, Fascism and religious asceticism, and escaping them both he revives but succumbs to a disease first diagnosed by Marx and announced by Marx himself at the end of the play: "The instruments of production have been too much for him. He is liquidated." This play reveals Auden yielding to Marxist influence but it is mixed up with his essentially psychological view of society. The chorus at the end of the play asserts that feudalism ended because agriculture barons could not understand "lending on credit," that the Middle Ages declined when sheep pastures replaced common grazing lands and when Luther and Calvin justified capitalism by inventing a religion.

While *Paid on Both Sides* and *The Dance of Death* contain both psychological and Marxist elements, *Look Stranger* (1935) is entirely Marxist. Auden here abandons, at least for the time being, the idea of psychological cure in favour of Marxist thesis, rejecting change of heart for a programme of political action. His Marxism by and large was in agreement with certain things held by Marxists: that social health demands a change of environment, that any policy of action is to be based on an empirical survey of facts and the value of action is to be measured by its consequences in satisfying human needs. Auden's essay "The Good Life" (1935)[19] also contained ideas not totally Marxist although they aligned him with the Marxist Left.

The founding of the Group Theatre in 1932 is an important landmark of the thirties since it constitutes a significant attempt to revive the stage. W.H. Auden, Christopher Isherwood, Stephen Spender, Rupert Doone and Robert Medley began to stage plays under its banner. Besides poets, musicians, painters and dancers were to collaborate in the production:

> Among the little experimental theatres which existed in England in the 1930's the Group Theatre occupies an important position not only because it first produced a number of new English politico-poetic plays, but also because the theatre wanted to realize an avant-garde idea of the total theatre, joining different arts into a synthetic whole. It attempted to diminish the alienation between actors and spectators, or rather, to annihilate the barrier preventing an active participation of the public in theatrical art.[20]

It is a total theatre in that it gives creativity the highest possible communication. The members of the Group Theatre wanted to have a trained company of actors who would work with a missionary zeal for the realization of certain programmes, political and social. Among the architects of the Group Theatre, there were Rupert Doone who had been trained in classical ballet and who had worked with Diaghilev, Robert Medley who was an expert maker of costumes, scenery and masks, Herbert Murrill, William Alwyn, Benjamin Britten, all musicians, Tyrone Guthrie, John Piper and Henry Moore. Auden's influence loomed large on the productions.

Julian Symons credits Auden and Rupert Doone with providing aesthetic scaffolding to the Group Theatre: "The Group Theatre had aesthetic ideas, and it had a social attitude, the first springing largely from Doone, the second from Auden.[21] The Group Theatre's manifesto was contained in Auden's "I want the Theatre To Be" in the programme issued by the *Westminster Theatre* at the production of *The Dance of Death* on October 1, 1935:

> The Drama began as the act of a whole community. Ideally there would be no spectators. In practice every member of the

audience should feel like an understudy.

Drama is essentially an art of the body. The basis of acting is acrobatics, dancing, and all forms of physical skill. The music hall, the Christmas pantomime, and the country house charade are the most living drama of today.

The development of the film has deprived drama of any excuse for being documentary. It is not in its nature to provide an ignorant passive spectator with exciting news.

The subject of drama on the other hand, is the commonly known, the universally familiar stories of the society or generation in which it is written. The audience, like the child listening to a fairy tale, ought to know what is going to happen next. Similarly drama is not suited to the analysis of character, which is the province of the novel. Dramatic characters are simplified, easily recognizable and over life-size.

Dramatic speech should have the same confessed, significant, and undocumentary character, as dramatic movement.

Drama in fact deals with the general and universal, not with the particular and local, but it is probable that drama can only deal, at any rate directly, with the relations of human beings with each other, not with the relation of man to the rest of nature.[22]

The ideas contained in Auden's manifesto although interesting are not completely new since Gordon Craig had very nearly said the same things: "Craig's vision of over life-size dramatic character ("Uebermarionette"), his rejection of realistic forms of drama, imitation of nature, and psychological interpretation of characters, were either consciously or unknowingly repeated."[23] Whether or not Auden borrowed from Craig his theory of drama and its performance shows his unmistakable predilection for the theatre as well as it expresses his discontent with the prevalent modes of performances. The Group Theatre initially put into practice some of Auden's ideas but they became popular with some avant-garde groups like the Living Theatre and the Royal Shakespeare Company in the 1960s.

Auden's dramatic concepts found enthusiasts as well as dissenters. The immediate contemporary response was negative. W.A. Darlington[24] and Derek Verschoyle[25] stated that Auden's ideas were historically inaccurate and not in the history of the European theatre. Ashley Dukes, director of the Mercury Theatre and a drama critic, was among those who defended Auden's concepts. Ivor Brown held the view that the Moscow Arts Theatre and English Little Theatres propagated these ideas already. Whether or not Auden's theory found favour with critics, it cannot be denied that it reflects more Auden's emotional, eruptive rejection of the existing theatrical conventions than a carefully conceived original programme and it represents an important rebellion against everything stale and outworn in drama and theatre: "It is clear though, that he wished not only to destroy old concepts but also to build a new vision of dramatic and theatrical art."[26] The radicalism that Auden was preaching would not have surprised those who had known him at Oxford.

Another important document relating to Auden's interest in theatre came in 1936 called "Selling the Group Theatre" or *Group Theatre Paper 1*, a summary of which is given by Mirko Jurak:

> It begins with the idea that art is relevant to man because it increases his understanding of life, strengthens his activity, and entertains. Later in the proclamation, Auden states that art becomes decadent if there were no live connections between it and the structure of social life. This kind of art is not arrived at automatically; it can be achieved only through struggle and experimentation. And in this he also sees the function of the experimental theatre, which may not be entirely successful commercially, but which is significant in the development of theatrical art. Auden compares scientific activity and experimental theatre, like the Group Theatre, and points out that both need support; and he mentions that the Theatre can show variety of efforts in cultural spheres and, therefore, he invites the audience to come and see the performances and become their patrons.[27]

Auden's proclamation presumably was meant to help Doone and

Medley who sought sustenance for their efforts from the public.

Stephen Spender, the youngest of the Auden Group, admired the daringly new ideas of the Group Theatre although his contribution to its dramaturgic policies was not much. Writing on the collaborations of Auden-Isherwood plays, he says:

> At present, the plays of Auden and Isherwood and the group of writers collaborating with the Group Theatre are experimental and they owe a great deal to Expressionism. Some of their devices, such as the soliloquy and the chorus, seem to be justified: the soliloquy because it represents the stream of secret or unconscious thought of the individual; the chorus because it expresses the generalized mood of a body of opinion at a certain time. But I believe that the writers of poetic drama will learn to do without improvisation as they build up a form which aims at a calm realism: a realism with a range of reference to contemporary problems and with an approach which can evade the surface naturalism of the drama and the whims of the censor.[28]

Himself a poet-playwright, Spender not only justifies the use of expressionistic devices by Auden, he himself employed them in his play *Trial of a Judge* (1938).

In spite of its radicalism manifest in the rejection of solo or star principle of acting, creation of homogeneous group of actors, popularization of the notion of total theatre, the Group Theatre had limited popularity in the thirties but its ideas were hailed with great enthusiasm after the Second World War. The Auden-Doone dramatic art failed to gain wider acceptance because the Group Theatre produced plays for a middle-class audience, which hadn't the slightest wish to participate in action. As Symons remarks, "The Group Theatre was never anything like the act of a whole community. It was a gesture made by middle-class radicals to a middle-class liberal audience."[29]

Auden's interest in the theatre is due not only to the influence of Brecht and the enthusiasm of Robert Medley and Rupert Doone but also to his awareness of the efficiency of drama as a means of projecting our image of human reality. In "Psychology and Art To-Day," (1935) Auden wrote: "You cannot tell people what to do; you can only tell them parables; and that is what art really is, particular stories of particular people and experiences, from which each according to his immediate and particular needs may draw his own conclusions."[30] His use of parables is attributable to his conviction that poetry could be a means of education and promotion of mental culture needed for achieving an effectual if not creative relation between his self and society of the world.

About the same time, Auden made the statement that "Poetry is not concerned with telling people what to do, but with expanding our knowledge of good and evil, perhaps making the necessity of action more urgent and its nature more clear, but only leading us to the point where it is possible for us to make a rational and moral choice."[31] Auden's statement draws attention to an inherent tendency of his poetry which is moralistic in its import without becoming didactic. It is drama rather than the novel which affords the means necessary to convey objective concepts to the mind of the audience which makes for the predominance of literary content in his plays. Interestingly, this sets off the practice of some of the avant garde dramatists who are concerned with the reducing of the literary content of the drama in the interests of the total theatre. The language of drama, it is worth noting, can transmit and intensify an image but cannot serve as a substitute for an image which is the reason why the characters in Auden's plays tend to be shadowy.

Auden went to the theatre, like W.B. Yeats and T.S. Eliot before him, to gain an audience and to perform social function for poetry. All the three felt that the theatre would reconcile and reunite the private world of the poet with the public world of the theatre. While Yeats attempted the assimilation of a true Celtic mythos to the common consciousness of his people, Eliot sought a revivification of the consciousness of contemporary man through the recognition of the "primordial affirmative." Significantly, Yeats's dream of a Celtic twilight was not translated into reality since the twilight dissolved into darkness rather than a new dawn but Eliot was able to realize a mythopoeic image of the human scene which, though suggestive of a kind of nihilistic terminus, is "redeemed" by his assertion of faith. Auden on the other hand was principally concerned with the endowment of the masses with a poetic imagination in order that they might redeem themselves in their own eyes if not of the world's. While Yeats seemed intent in the interests of nationalism on quickening people into a new awareness of thei· destiny, Eliot and Auden had no such avowed purposes.

Auden realized that the middle-classes constituted his real audience and hence his insistence on the adaptations of the techniques of music hall and Christmas pantomime to the familiar dramatic conventions. Referring to the failure of Yeats and other poetic dramatists, Auden wrote: "The truth is that those who would write poetic drama, refuse to start from the only place where they can start, from the dramatic forms already in use . . . the thriller, the drama of ideas, the comedy of manners, and, standing somewhat eccentrically to these, the ballet. . . . Poetic drama should start with the stock musical comedy characters—the rich uncle, the vamp, the mother-in-law, the sheik, and so forth—and make them, as only poetry can, memorable. . . . If the would-be poetic dramatist . . . is willing to be humble and sympathetic, to accept what he finds to his hand and develop its latent possibilities, he may be agreeably surprised to find that after all the public will stand, may even enjoy, a good deal of poetry."[32] Auden argued in support of revue and musical comedy on the ground that the stock characters of musical comedy have some psychological and symbolic value. This is an indication of Auden's eagerness to absorb the full range of literary tradition that would draw the extremes—the aristocrat and the peasant—closer and his readiness to educate an audience as one belonging to them not as one different from them. In *The Dog Beneath the Skin*, Auden combines musical comedy and the choruses.

The plays that Auden wrote in collaboration with Christopher Isherwood contained both prose and verse but they are not so successful as Eliot's poetic dramas for the simple reason that the Group Theatre's productions were faulty. Nevertheless, the plays were successful because the plays attracted the audience more by entertainment than by piety. Their popularity proved that it was possible to interest an audience in a type of play rather resembling the revue or even the musical comedy. Aristotelian development of character and conflict was not attempted in plays like *The Dog Beneath the Skin* or *On the Frontier* but in all the plays the dramatists employ soliloquies, choruses, homilies etc. The absence of character development and conflict has led critics to label Auden-Isherwood plays "schematic construction." While John Bradbury describes them as "dramatic without being drama,"[33] Spears remarks that they are "fables, modern morality plays; they are intended to appeal to the minds and not to the emotions of the audience."[34] It is perhaps true that Auden was more interested in ideas and the characters who represented them rather than characters who represented emotions. Just as in poetry he arranges a confrontation between two differing and opposing ideas, in the plays he arranges a confrontation between characters representing ideas.

Auden's plays like *The Dog Beneath the Skin* make use of cinematic techniques of composition. In his poetry there is a "montage" of social observations, the poems proceed neither by the juxtaposition of symbolic image, nor by ratiocination. The sonnet "Petition" shows Auden's montage of social observations. The rationale behind the selection of images is to demonstrate a thesis. Taken separately these images lack concreteness but "together they create the effect of marvellous taut accuracy that is the hall-mark of Auden's best poetry."[35] The Russian cinema of Dovzhenko, Pudovkin and Eisenstein appears to have been an important influence upon the young Auden because it was remarkable in the evocation of socio-political atmosphere of disparate yet relevantly selected shots—by montage. Auden's use of cinematic technique of structuring of his poetry seems necessitated by his interest in presenting a moving image rather than a static one which has the added advantage of realizing within the confines of his poetry the rhythms of human impulses. The scenic movement characterizing his poetic drama is an objectification of the instinctive drives of man underlying the patterns of his behaviour.

In *The Dog Beneath the Skin* (1935), *The Ascent of F6* (1936) and *On the Frontier* (1938), the playwrights attempt an evocation of socio-political pictures in a series of montage sequences. Alan

Norman's quest in *The Dog* for the missing heir of Pressan Ambo lands him in states where civic disorder and political barbarism is the rule. In a montage sequence, the vulgarity of modern civilization is presented. It is a play which has all the ideas that engaged Auden's imagination and the imagination of the thirties's generation. Governments and ideologies come in for severe criticism. Totalitarianism, Authoritarianism, Fascism have been pictured. As for the Marxist material, the author's use of it is superficial. The opening chorus introduces the familiar Marxist idea, "Man is changed by his living." In the scene set in a lunatic asylum, the authors defend communism against the familiar charge that it subordinates the individual to the state. In the last line of the play, the familiar slogan from *The Communist Manifesto* is rephrased: "To each his need: from each his power." In spite of the Marxist colouring, *The Dog* is not entirely Marxist.

The Ascent of F6 has a mosaic of themes—psychological, political, philosophical and religious. The play owes its significance less to its topicality than to the profundity of the questions dealt by it. Michael Ransom, the exceptional man, in agreeing to scale "the Haunted Mountain" becomes a victim of mother-fixation and in choosing a course of action for his followers, plays a corrupt and spurious role of a saviour. It may be that in Ransom "Auden was delineating a double contradiction that he knew threatened himself: the contradiction between an artist's work and his beliefs, and the contradiction between the public pursuit of fame and the private neurosis that makes it so fatally attractive. These contradictions are especially harrowing to an artist, for even when he most wants to write about his personal psychology, he is constrained to keep it secret from his public if he hopes to maintain their approval. A mountaineer's triumph seems rather less impressive if he announces that he conquered his peak neither for England nor because it was there, but because it symbolized his mother's inaccessible breast."[36]

Ransom's undertaking which is to climb the Haunted Mountain might appear foolhardy but in the context of the play it provides a deepening perspective in which human endeavour itself could be investigated. The hunting for motives can be frustrating as this play demonstrates, since Auden's purpose is not to present any psychological case history as such but to "evaluate" human behaviour considered in such striking but representative contexts as is projected in the play. One, therefore, while appreciating a view like that of Mendelson, might like to reserve his judgement. To suggest as Mendelson has done that to Ransom the mountain symbolizes the inaccessible breast of his mother is to invoke a Freudian approach which cannot be asserted without relating it to the play of the Oedipal complex. The fact that the play has an open ending expressive of the indeterminacy of human motivation although the unveiling of the mother by Ransom might be regarded as the unmasking of a deep-seated sub-conscious drive like the Oedipal or an instinctual drive like that of filial piety.

On the Frontier, last of the collaborative plays, was preceded by *Letter to Lord Byron* which is grounded in his immediate concerns as a member of a society which is the reason why the focus of the poem is his own particular situation as an Englishman and English poet, the awareness of which makes for an expansion of consciousness. The poem, therefore, does not express such characteristic public concerns as depression, unemployment, hunger marches, dole queues, industrial ruins. But "Spain 1937" written in the same year has the freedom-necessity choice formula Auden got from Marx and Engels. Dealing ostensibly with the Spanish Civil War in which communists were involved, this poem remains aloof from partisanship but returns to the philosophical basis of Marxism. *On the Frontier* is a Marxist play centering not only on the Marxist interpretation of history but also on the implications of the historical acceleration that Marxism has come to spell: "It dramatizes the dialectical leap Marx had foretold, the historical moment when capitalist society, crumbling under its own internal pressures, gives way to a proletarian uprising."[37]

II

The year 1939 is a significant one in Auden's personal life and literary career. It is the year which 'divides' his work and life into two equal halves—seemingly suggestive of the translation of the

Englishman into an American with all the attendant consequences which came to be highlighted with appreciable critical ingenuity. For one thing it came to be viewed as a great divide in order to account for the transitions in his poetry and in his beliefs. It is probably difficult to establish that the very Englishness of his writings and of his convictions has given place to what could be identified with the American if considered in terms of the concept of Americanness.

Auden's migration to America caused bitterness among his admirers and sparked off a controversy which was to become a theme in critical writings for the next two decades. His return to the church soon after was looked upon as an act of "betrayal" of the Marxist cause and an abandonment of his earlier social commitment. That Auden buried the messianic hopes he had vested in direct action was manifest in certain coincidences: Grigson who established *New Verse* obviously to bring about a revolution under Auden's leadership wound up soon after the latter's departure; The Group Theatre, founded to serve as a vehicle for Auden's and Isherwood's popular drama, faded away deprived of hope and sustenance. Cyril Connolly and John Lehman saw in Auden's migration the formal burial of the Thirties movement. Others assumed that Auden was scared of the coming war and concluded that, once again in Left-wing history, the leader deserted the troops.

The protesting voices against Auden's migration were many: "Resentment of Auden as a Lost Leader was an obvious motive, though rarely an ostensible one, in much criticism of the later thirties and forties, and it still survives."[38] A number of essays written on Auden's emigration and reconversion began to point out "inverted development" in the artistic career of the poet. The enthusiasm with which Leavis initially greeted Auden's work soon gave way to a kind of disillusionment evidenced by his not holding out any hope for Auden. This might be attributed to his sensing of a weakening of the poetic impulse or a slackening of his control over the "singing line," though not to any appreciable decline in Auden's poetic powers.

The stand taken by Leavis and the *Scrutiny* was strengthened by critics like Randall Jarrell[39] and Joseph Warren Beach.[40] Refuting

Jarrell and Beach, Spears contends that the "rapidly shifting beliefs" of Auden were confined to one brief period in the late thirties, that they were all in the same direction, and that, once the fundamental commitment to Christianity had been fully made, the only changes were mere shifts of emphasis."[41] One would like to add that the seeming shifts of Auden's stand or the transitions from a Marxist to a Christian stance derive from an implicit conviction that godlessness is "an ontological impossibility for man," that there is an undeniable continuity between the created man and the reborn man of faith—a conviction which he seems to share with Karl Barth.

More recently the controversy centering on migration and conversion has been played down. In fact, Auden's American years are now considered more fruitful because up there Auden wrote his brilliant long poems *For the Time Being* (1944), *The Sea and the Mirror* (1944), *The Age of Anxiety* (1947), not to speak of shorter poems like "In Praise of Limestone" and critical essays on a variety of themes. Although the debate has died down, the issues raised continued to attract academic attention. (The interesting aspect of the controversy is that Auden never interposed in it but kept his cool unagitated and unprovoked. Probably the reasons were far too many and far too private to mention in public.) One interesting view in this regard is that of Hoggart: "He (Auden) has deliberately cut himself off from the ties of family, race and the English scene, all of which meant much to him. He is alone in a crowd. He left partly out of disgust with the mess England had made of her affairs in the thirties, but more importantly *for reasons connected with his art.*"[42] If Auden's departure to America indeed was "for reasons connected with his art," it would be tantamount to sad reflection on the state of poetry in England and what is more would hardly explain his return to his country. It therefore seems futile to speculate about the reasons for leaving this country except to suggest that he might have felt the need of a kind of psychological distancing to perspectivize the human scene unencumbered by old loyalties or commitments. Such an impression seems not unwarranted because as reported by Cyril Connolly: "He (Auden) reverts always to the same argument, that a writer needs complete anonymity, he must break away from the European literary happy family . . . and he must reconsider all the family values.''[43]

In an interview, Auden gave reasons for his choice of America: ''The attractiveness of America to a writer is its openness and lack of tradition. In a way it is frightening. You are forced to live here as everyone else will be forced to live. There is no past. No tradition. No roots—that is, in the European sense. . . . But what is happening here is happening everywhere. The general effect of the trends of machinery has been to de-root people. . . . With history moving so fast, people are so afraid: People feel, what is the permanent thing?''[44] Auden's choice of America, if juxtaposed with Eliot's choice of England, would spell an interesting perspective on this question which cannot be resolved in terms which have been proposed by some of the critics. Seemingly, their choice was dictated by identical considerations which, if true, would present both of them in deplorable light. The inescapable conclusion is that their decisions to quit the land of their birth stemmed from mystical reasons which are inaccessible to intellectual cognition.

Although it is futile to speculate on the reasons for Auden's migration, an examination of the social and political conditions at the time of Auden's migration may not be totally unwarranted. Many artists and intellectuals were disillusioned by the cataclysmic events that occurred towards the end of the thirties. Their hope in secular earthly paradise based on a liberal belief in the goodness of man, their vision of absolute good society above power politics, and their hope of preventing another world war proved illusions. In Auden's case, they appear to have undermined his political optimism. He was obviously disappointed by the role played by his own country in European affairs: ''The England of his own earlier vision no longer existed, since the vision itself no longer existed; therefore, it became necessary to find a new country, in fact a new world, as context for the new and increased sense of uprooted isolation, of distance from the earlier 'local detail' that had given momentary meaning to experience.''[45]

Auden's decision to move to America with its ''synonymous cities besotted with electric signs,'' to make New York ''this world's most notoriously alienating metropolis,'' his new home could be appreciated in the context of his utterances soon after the emigration. In *New Year Letter,* which was read as a "public explanation of what to many in wartime England seemed a kind of defection,"[46] Auden says:

> More even than in Europe, here,
> The choice of patterns is made clear
> Which the machine imposes, what
> Is possible and what is not
> To what conditions we must bow
> In building the Just City now.[47]

It may be said that Auden was not the only one to be drawn towards New York. Lorca Mayakovsky, Hart Crane and a few others had gone there although the reasons for such a choice might not have been identical. In the introduction to *Faber Book of Modern American Verse,* Auden says: "In America... to move on and make a fresh start somewhere else is still the normal reaction to dissatisfaction or failure. Such social fluidity has important psychological effects. Since movement involves breaking social and personal ties, the habit creates an attitude toward personal relationships in which impermanence is taken for granted. . . . To be able at any time to break with the past, to move and keep on moving lessens the significance not only of the past but also of the future which is reduced to the immediate future, and minimizes the importance of political action."[48] In the light of these observations, it might be said that Auden was probably seeking a psychological distancing so as to perspectivize not only the human scene as a whole but also his own role in it.

As regards conversion, it seems necessary to answer criticism which says that Auden declared his faith in Christianity abruptly and that his reasons for it are far from convincing. Auden's own account of the matter is revealing. In an untitled essay in *Modern Canterbury Pilgrims,* Auden describes the devout Anglo-Catholic atmosphere of his home. His first religious memories are of "exciting magical rites" rather than of listening to sermons. He was also accustomed to doctrinal and liturgical controversy from his earliest years, and grew up with a uniquely Anglican conception of the church as a "community in which wide divergences of doctrine and rite can and do exist without leading necessarily to schism and excommunication."[49]

After his confirmation at thirteen, he appears to have lost interest in church and belief. Auden retrospectively regrets it: "I sometimes wonder, for example, what would have happened if, when I was at school or the University, a god parent or friend had given me the works of Kierkegaard or Rudolf Kassner, both of whom were, later in my life, destined to play a great part. The only theological writer I knew of at that time whom I found readable and disturbing to my complacency was Pascal."[50] Auden repeatedly acknowledges his debt to Rudolf Kassner and Kierkegaard in his religious development. Kassner's *Zahl Und Gesicht* was, Auden admits, one of those few books that had so conditioned his vision of life that he could not imagine who he was before he read them.

Auden refers to two continuing religious influences in his youth. He was born at a time when every educated youth was expected to know the Bible thoroughly and no undergraduate could take a degree without passing a Divinity examination. He sang in his school choirs and appeared to have enjoyed services in His worship. Ursula Niebuhr, who shared very much the same sort of English and Edwardian childhood as Auden, with a doctor father and a devout mother like Auden's, recalls how she and Auden had been influenced by Anglican liturgy: "Wystan sometimes became very nostalgic for the nineteenth-century hymns of our childhood and would go to the piano and rapturously play and sing loudly from Hymns Ancient and Modern."[51]

Recalling Auden's interest in Christian theology and commenting on Auden's review of Reinhold Niebuhr's *Christianity and Power Politics*, Ursula says that "the theological stance of Wystan seems to have been both definite and consistent."[52] According to her, Auden was reading in 1941 Tillich's *The Interpretation of History* and the novels of Kafka. Those who read some of his reviews were "intrigued" by his theological stance. Some academic theologians and some clergy felt "flattered" that a well-known poet would read theology but were "puzzled" by his free use of theological categories. Auden himself states: "I think my theological position is very much the same as Reinhold's, i.e., Augustinian, not Thomist. . . . Liturgically, I am Anglo-Catholic though not too spiky, I hope."[53]

Auden's reading of Reinhold Niebuhr appears to have deepened his interest in the history of Christian thought. Besides reviewing Niebuhr's *The Nature and Destiny of Man* (1941), he also reviewed with him C.N. Cochrane's *Christianity and Classical Culture: A Study of Thought and Action from Augustus to Augustine*. Among the books that Auden mentions as valuable are Charles Williams's *Forgiveness of Sins* and *Descent of the Dove*. After reading and rereading the latter for sixteen years, Auden seems to have found it "a source of intellectual delight and spiritual nourishment which remains inexhaustible."[54]

A friend and contemporary of Auden at Oxford, Anne Fremantle, who had turned a Roman Catholic at the same time as Auden's conversion, reports her meeting with him in 1943 on which occasion he told her: "I was always very lucky with God. . . . I was a choirboy, and so I always enjoyed singing, and I was a boat boy. So even when I got bored with God, I always enjoyed his worship."[55]

John Auden, the poet's elder brother, mentions the twin events of the War and the death of their mother behind Auden's return to religion: "In August 1941 our mother died in England while Wystan was in New York and I in Calcutta. He said that he could never open those few of her letters which arrived after her death . . . Golo Mann has suggested that Wystan's sudden return to religion may have been influenced by Reinhold Niebuhr's *The Nature and Destiny of Man*. This is quite possibly so but Wystan told me after the war that the primary reason was our mother's death, and he once more accepted the Anglo-Catholicism of his childhood."[56] Although Auden returned to Church a good ten months before his mother's death, the distress caused by it appears to have made him hold fast to it for the rest of his life as is evidenced by his writing *For the Time Being* and its dedication to the memory of his mother.

Auden describes three personal experiences which occurred between 1937-40. During the Spanish Civil War, Auden found the churches closed and not a priest was seen. This discovery left him profoundly shocked and disturbed. He held that though he had consciously ignored and rejected the church for sixteen years, the existence of churches and what went on in them had all the time been very important to him. Auden recalls meeting during that time "an Anglican layman, and for the first time in my life felt myself in the presence of personal sanctity. I had met many good people before who made me feel ashamed of my shortcomings, but in the presence of this man . . . I felt transformed into a person who was incapable of doing or thinking anything base or unloving. I later discovered that he had a similar effect on many other people."[57] The Anglican layman that Auden mentions is Charles Williams, who seemed to have wrought similar changes in T.S. Eliot, C.S. Lewis and Dorothy Sayers.

Two important thinkers who seemed to have exercised considerable influence on Auden's thought in the forties were Kierkegaard and Niebuhr. Kierkegaard's emphasis on the individual soul, its suffering and arrival at faith and the importance of moral choice, Niebuhr's discussion of the conflict between freedom and necessity and the precise nature of sin, appeared to have appealed to Auden in forming his religious beliefs. Though explicit references to Christian ideas began to be made after his migration, they might be noticeable in the work of the thirties. Prayers, invocations, humility before an unknown God appears in poems and plays of that time. There is throughout a call for a "change of heart," a vision of the "Good Place" and the search for the place of "Love." Such a plea betokens an apprehension of relativism finding its historical resolution in the Absoluteness of Decision viz for or against Christ, Yes or No to God. Auden's Leftist attitude may be traced to his recognition that any quest of truth should begin with Reason, Being and Existence, the disregarding of which would render even theology irrelevant. The existentialist view that truth begins in existential self-analysis would appeal to an artist like Auden with his insistence on creative self-interpretation in art, since he seems aware of what Rudolf Bultmann asserted viz that even theology must begin with the existential description of man. But it should be obvious that Auden's is not an unqualified existential imagination as Sartre's or Kafka's. He, like Eliot, has however used myths in a manner suggestive of what Nathan Scott had indicated in his *Modern Literature and the Religious Frontier*—myths like the Myth of Hell, Myth of Sanctity.

The influence of Kierkegaard is deeper than any as is evident in Auden's work. He says:

> So, presently, I started to read some theological works, Kierkegaard in particular and began going, in a tentative and experimental sort of way, to church. And then, providentially—for the occupational disease of poets is frivolity—I was forced to know in person what it is like to feel oneself the prey of demonic powers, in both the Greek and the Christian sense, stripped of self-control and self-respect, behaving like a ham actor in a Strindberg play.[58]

Auden observes that Kierkegaard's talent lies in making Christianity sound bohemian. He comments:

> As a spirit, a conscious person endowed with free will, every man has, through faith and grace, a unique "existential" relation to God, and few since St. Augustine have described this relation more profoundly than Kierkegaard. But every man has a second relation to God which is neither unique nor existential: as a creature composed of matter, as a biological organism, every man, in common with everything else in the universe, is related by necessity to the God who created that universe and saw that it was good, for the laws of nature to which, whether he likes it or not, he must conform are of divine origin.[59]

Auden is drawn to Kierkegaardian existentialism not because it is opposed to Cartesian dualism and Hegelian idealism but because it takes in its sweep diverse ideas drawn from Nietzsche, Bergson, William James, Freud and Marx which have come to condition the intellectual climate of his age and which have come to emphasize that truth is the way deep inwardness. It may be seen that Kierkegaard's writings have had the effect of confronting him with issues of which he has had only a dim intimation—issues which seem to define the characteristic temper and tenor of his age. Auden's reading of his age, an age of anxiety, is derived from the premises underlying the diverse structures of thought like those of the above-mentioned thinkers which attempt to bring out the substratum of man's self and being in order that man's existential predicament might be analyzed. Like the existentialists, Auden does not believe in the so-called eternal verities but regards all truth as being relative to the being of man.

Critics like Edward Callan have suggested that the Kierkegaardian categories of the aesthetic, ethical and religious have been employed by Auden as a structural principle in his long poems. For instance, *For the Time Being* (1944) is Kierkegaardian in that it defines the significance of the birth of Christ not in terms of the so-called Christian verities but in those expressive of the "witnessing" of Christ. *The New Year Letter* (1941) and *The Age of Anxiety* (1947) are predicated on such problems as freedom of the will, of evil, of sin considered in terms of the existentialist description of man not in those of traditional Christological terms.

It may thus be seen that in all Auden's works, there runs a current of thought related to the deepening or broadening of the living experiential dimensions of Christian faith in order that a new vitality might be infused into the Christian life. However, if Eliot's categories as discussed in his essay "Religion and Literature" are applied to Auden's writings they cannot be termed religious works at all since they seem more concerned with the demythologizing rather than the rationalizing of the Christian Message in order to bring the spiritual or the religious closer to the empirical without having recourse to the postulates of empirical theology. In other words they seek to interpret the constellation of events in man's life in the manner not of process theology but that of Christian pragmatism:

> the dominant feature of Auden's conversion is paradoxically, its element of continuity with his secular past. The whole process is very different from the popular notion of violent

> and sudden change, a Pauline stroke of lightning on the road to Damascus. . . . Nevertheless, it is striking that in terms both of his ideas and of his emotional attitudes, Auden's conversion suggests not a sudden break but a change of key in old ideas which, basically, live on.[60]

It may be added that Auden has undergone no "conversion," sudden or otherwise, as Paul or Augustine but only as experience with an increasing intensity of conviction his own predilections for what might be termed "authentic" existence viz. the life in faith.

NOTES

1. Daniel Hoffman, ed., *Harvard Guide to Contemporary American Poetry* (New York: Oxford Univesity Press, 1979), p. 458.
2. *Ibid.*, p. 54.
3. Stephen Spender, "Valediction," *W.H. Auden: A Tribute*, ed. Stephen Spender (New York: MacMillan, 1975), p. 245.
4. Frank Kermode, *Modern Essays* (London: Collins, 1971), p. 347.
5. Francois Duchene, *The Case of the Helmeted Airman* (London: Chatto and Windus, 1972), p. 60.
6. *Ibid.*, p. 61.
7. *The English Auden*, ed. Edward Mendelson (London: Faber, 1977), p. 245.
8. Reviewing the last four books A. Walton Litz ("Revisiting the Thirties," *Sewanee Review*, 87 (1979), pp. 660-66) suggests that one must go beyond the four books for a balanced historical view of English literature in the 1930s. He considers Samuel Hynes's *The Auden Generation* (1976) as "a model of sequential literary history" and Symons's book "a survivor's view of his own literary generation . . . remarkably undistorted by sentiment or a self-justifying need to revise the past."
9. The fantasy world created by Isherwood and his friend Edward Upward consisted of a fantastic village, "a sort of anarchist paradise in which all accepted moral and social values were turned upside down and inside out and every kind of extravagant behaviour was possible and usual. It was our private place of retreat from the rules

9. and conventions of University life." Christopher Isherwood, quoted in Samuel Hynes, *The Auden Generation* (London: The Bodley Head, 1976), p. 35.
10. Julian Symons, *The Thirties: A Dream Revolved* (London: Faber, 1960), p. 35.
11. Day Lewis, *The Buried Day* (London: Chatto and Windus, 1960), p. 216.
12. Stephen Spender, *The Thirties and After: Poetry, Politics, People 1933-1970* (New York: Random House, 1978), p.8.
13. *New Verse*, 26-27 (November 1937), p. 9.
14. Stephen Spender, *The Thirties and After*, p. 10.
15. Stephen Spender, "W.H. Auden and His Poetry," *Auden: Twentieth-Century Views*, ed. Monroe K. Spears (Englewood Cliffs, New Jersey: Prentice Hall, 1964), p. 27.
16. Frederick Buell, *W.H. Auden as a Social Poet* (New York: Carnell University Press, 1973), p. 87.
17. Breon Mitchell, "W.H. Auden and Christopher Isherwood: The 'German Influence'," *Oxford German Studies*, 1 (1966), p. 165.
18. Frederick Buell, p. 96.
19. *The English Auden*, pp. 342-52.
20. Mirko Jurak, "Dramaturgic Concepts of the English Group Theatre: The Totality of the Artistic Achievement," *Modern Drama*, 16 (June 1973), p. 81.
21. Julian Symons, p. 76.
22. Mirko Jurak, p. 82.
23. *Loc. cit.*
24. *Ibid.*, p. 83.
25. Derek Verschoyle, "The Theatre," *The Spectator* (Oct. 11, 1935), p. 547.
26. Mirko Jurak, p. 83.
27. *Ibid.*, p. 85.
28. Stephen Spender, "Poetry and Expressionism," *The New Statesman* (March 12, 1938), p. 409.
29. Julian Symons, p. 77.
30. *The English Auden*, p. 341.
31. *Ibid.*, p. 329.
32. Edward Mendelson, *Early Auden* (London: Faber, 1981), p. 262.
33. John Bradbury, "Auden and the Tradition," *Western Review*, 12 (Summer 1948), p. 229.
34. Monroe K Spears, *The Poetry of W.H. Auden: The Disenchanted*

Island (New York: Oxford University Press, 1963), p. 91.

35. Geoffrey Thurley, *The Ironic Harvest* (London: Edward Arnold, 1974), p. 60.
36. *Early Auden*, p. 285.
37. Justin Replogle, "Auden's Marxism," *PMLA*, 80, 5 (1965), p. 591.
38. M.K. Spears, *Auden*, p. 1.
39. Randall Jarrell, "Changes of Attitude and Rhetoric in Auden's Poetry," *The Southern Review*, 7 (1941), pp. 326-49; "Freud to Paul: The Stages of Auden's Ideology," *Partisan Review*, 12 (1945), pp. 437-57.
40. Joseph Warren Beach, *The Making of the Auden Canon* (Minneapolis: University of Minnesota Press, 1957).
41. Spears, *Auden*, p. 3.
42. Richard Hoggart, *Auden: An Introductory Essay* (London: Chatto and Windus, 1951), p. 136.
43. Quoted in Richard Hoggart, p. 136.
44. *Ibid.*, p. 137.
45. Barbara Everett, *Auden* (London: Oliver and Boyd, 1964), p. 69.
46. John Fuller, *A Reader's Guide to W.H. Auden* (London: Thames and Hudson, 1970), p. 132.
47. *Collected Longer Poems* (London: Faber, 1968), p. 125.
48. Barbara Everett, p. 70.
49. *Modern Canterbury Pilgrims*, ed. James A. Pike (New York: Morehouse-Gorham, 1956), quoted in Spears, p. 173.
50. *Loc. cit.*
51. Ursula Niebuhr, "Memories of the 1940s," *W.H. Auden: A Tribute*, ed. Stephen Spender (London: Weidenfeld and Nicholson, 1975), p. 104.
52. *W.H. Auden: A Tribute*, p. 104.
53. *Ibid.*, p. 106.
54. Quoted in Spears, p. 176.
55. Anne Fremantle, "Reality and Religion," *W.H. Auden: A Tribute*, p. 89.
56. John Auden, "A Brother's View Point." *Ibid.*, p. 28.
57. Introduction to *Modern Canterbury Pilgrims*, quoted in Spears, p. 173.
58. *Modern Canterbury Pilgrims*, p. 41.
59. Spears, *The Poetry of Auden*, p. 177.
60. Francois Duchene, *The Case of the Helmeted Airman* (London: Chatto and Windus, 1972), p. 154.

Paid on Both Sides: A Charade

W.H. Auden's first attempt at drama *Paid on Both Sides* is called a "charade." Written during his stay in Berlin in 1928, it was justifiably regarded as a verse play of an unusual kind which indisputably exercised considerable influence on the poetic drama of the thirties. This "dauntingly obscure" charade first appeared in T.S. Eliot's Quarterly *The Criterion* for January 1930. Eliot could not conceal his enthusiasm for the young Auden and his brilliant work. He wrote to E. Mcknight Kauffer: "I have sent you the new *Criterion* to ask you to read a verse play *Paid on Both Sides*, by a young man I know, which seems to me a brilliant piece of work. . . . This fellow is about the best poet that I have discovered in several years." The interest in Auden's experimental work was not confined to Eliot alone. It was shared among others by such distinguished contemporaries of his as William Empson who wrote an illuminating analysis of his work, although he came to make fun of its ominous note and sense of impending doom.[1]

The distinctiveness of *Paid on Both Sides* is discernible if compared to *Transitional Poem* by Cecil Day Lewis to whom it was dedicated. While Lewis's poem is cast in the traditional mould, Auden's work is unmistakably modern in that it is "elliptical and knotted in its style, ambiguously located in time and space, unstable and untraditional in its mixture of tragedy, lyricism, and farce."[2] Considered in this perspective, Auden's *Paid on Both Sides* seems to be "more completely imagined, more fully realized in action and metaphor, more clearly an alternative world"[3] than Lewis's poem. Ostensibly concerned with hereditary feuds, *Paid on Both Sides* projects an alarming vision of the English bourgeoise class facing its gravest crisis of history. This is attributable to both a belief in the

Marxist apocalypse and the Germanism of the poet's sensibility which is not surprising in view of Auden having lived in Germany in the last days of Weimar Republic which witnessed the rise of Hitler to power. To the conventionally minded readers, such a work as this would be embarrassing since no well-known poet would so obviously present the contemporary reality. Moreover, Auden being the son of a doctor was interested in investigating the ills of his own age and his distinction lies in extending as it were what might be termed "psychosomatic diagnosis" to the political and socio-cultural realms of the nation's being. Faced with the frightening problems of his time Auden like any other intellectual turned to Marxism, although what resulted from it was only an emotional attitude rather than a philosophy of life. Indeed, there was no commitment on his part to Marxist creed or credo since to his generation Freud and Marx were as Luther and Calvin would be to the religious minded intellectuals.

Though called a charade, *Paid on Both Sides* cannot be strictly considered a charade at all since it attempts a fictional engineering that cannot be accommodated within the formal confines of a charade. As Hynes points out, a charade is "a theatrical form distinguished by three features: it is private—for the entertainment of a small group of persons who know each other; it is a game; and it is non-realistic—in a charade, the actions carry meanings that are not literally representational."[4] Auden's thematic interest in *so far* as this work is concerned cannot be realized through the simplistic dramatic procedures characteristic of the charade—an interest which posits a plot that combines the pro-airetic and the hermeneutic needed for winning credence for his view. As might be seen in this work, the hermeneutic overshadows the pro-airetic since it is not the completion of an action logically derived from its initiation but the revelation of meaning that matters most to him. It is interesting that an entry in 1929 Journal reads: "The Tyranny of the Dead. One cannot react against them."[5] To consider *Paid on Both Sides* as "a study in that Tyranny,"[6] as Edward Mendelson has done, is to identify one of the principal thematic strands in the work in order to investigate its insidious working in the life of the hero of the play John Nower. Moreover, Auden's interest in exploring this phenomenon is not confined to the presentation of the workings of the ancestral curse or the tyranny of the dead but extends to the considerations of such questions as psychological restraints genetically transmitted and such other psycho-physiological inhibiting factors operating in the human milieu.

The charade begins with the premature birth of John Nower while Joan, his mother, is reeling under the shock of her husband's death at the hands of the enemy family. The feud between the Nowers and the Shaws is hereditary and ageless. Joan appears with the new-born child on the one side and the corpse of her husband on the other side. The death of her husband does not indicate the end of the feud but instead a continuation is signalled in the birth of her son. In slightly obscure lines of the first quatrain, she indicates her son's role in the predetermined and painful future of revenge and counter-revenge:

> Not from this life, not from this life is any
> To keep; sleep, day and play would not help there,
> Dangerous to new ghost: new ghost learns from many,
> Learns from old termers what death is, where. (12)[7]

She resolves that her son pursue " unforgetting vengeance," and wills that his "new ghost" learn from "old termers what death is, where." The morning of Nower's birth is to be an "unforgiving morning," which will bind the future to old hatreds:

> Unforgetting is not today's forgetting
> For yesterday, not bedrid scorning,
> But a new begetting,
> An unforgiving morning (13)

In the opening scene of this play, Auden has tried to compress the action in the gnomic manner of Joan's speech which, as Fuller suggests, he seems to have picked from Laura Riding.[8] The condensed time-scale of the first scene puts the feud into perspective and points out the transition from the peace attempts of John's father to the hypnotic and insidious call to arms by Joan.

Joan's address is followed by the chorus which responds in an admonishing tone observing that the young "brought forward into light/For warm dark moan" are prepared to be guided by the elders till they are dead but however very soon realize that they are mistaken:

Can speak of trouble, pressure on men
Born all the time, brought forward into light
For warm dark moan.
Though heart fears all heart cries for, rebuffs with mortal beat
Skyfall, the legs sucked under, adder's bite.
That prize held out of reach
Guides the unwilling tread,
The asking breath,
Till on attended bed
Or in untracked dishonour comes to each
His natural death. . . .

We were mistaken, these faces are not ours.
They smile no more when we smile back:
Eyes, ears, tongue, nostrils bring
News of revolt, inadequate counsel to
An infirm king.

O watcher in the dark, you wake
Our dream of waking, we feel
Your finger on the flesh that has been skinned,
By your bright day
See clear what we were doing, that we were vile.
Your sudden hand
Shall humble great
Pride, break it, wear down to stumps old systems which await
The last transgression of the sea. (13-14)

Once they realize that they are betrayed, the young begin to recognize a greater power ("watcher in the dark") which arouses the will to awake to a different order of reality and which proposes clear standards of morality and humility lacking in the "old systems which await/The last transgression of the sea."

In the second scene, John Nower appears in his youthfulness. Twenty years elapsed. Dick, Nower's friend, obviously sick of the feud, is planning to emigrate: "I have thought it all over and I think it is the best thing to do. . . . I don't know how I shall like the Colonies but I feel I must get away from here. There is not room enough . . . but the actual moving is unpleasant." (14) He makes a choice which will liberate him from the primitive habits of bloodthirsty acts and from the parental authority. John Nower, like Dick, can migrate and begin a new life. Like the quest hero who hears the call, John Nower hears Dick's call for migration but refuses to act. On the other hand, he is preparing his men to attack his enemy, Red Shaw at Brandon Walls. He discusses with George the strategy of attack: "I shall come with you. Let's see: it's dark now about five. Fortunately there's no moon and it's cloudy. We'll start then about half-past. Pick your men and get some sandwiches made up in the kitchen. I'll see about the ammunition if you will remember to bring a compass." (15) Nower's acton is directed by the psychological motive to replace his father in his mother's affections. The spell cast by his mother is so strong that he fails to be a moral being.

While John Nower is away to ambush Red Shaw, his men Kurt, Culley, Walter and Trudy get together for a drink and begin to talk about sports, the oncoming Christman and Nower. The world they picture is part schoolboy and part saga which suggests that the setting is partly fixed in time and partly transcendent. The setting is modern northern England but its code recollects the sagas and their gangster-ethic from an ancient past. The language is a mixture of schoolboy slang and alliterative Old English pastiche.

It is not only John Nower who acts according to the dictates of his ancestors, his men are similarly acting against their true selves. Trudy, for example, says:

> I am sick of this feud. What do we want to go on killing each
> other for?
> We are all the same. . . .

But here no remedy
Is to be thought of, no news but the new death;
A Nower dragged out in the night, a Shaw
Ambushed behind the wall. Blood on the ground
Would welcome fighters. . . .

I am old,
Shall die before next winter, but more than once shall hear
The cry for help, the shooting round the house. (17)

Walter supplements Trudy:

The best are gone.
Often the man, alone shut, shall consider
The killings in old winters, death of friends.
Sitting with stranger shall expect no good.

Spring came, urging to ships, a casting off,
But one would stay, vengeance not done, it seemed
Doubtful to them that they would meet again. . . .

I will say this not falsely; I have seen
The just and the unjust die in the day,
All, willing or not, and some were willing. (17)

The speeches of Trudy and Walter offer a comment on a characteristic feature of human predicament. Even before they complete their "dirge like rumination," John Nower returns after successfully avenging his father's death and reports:

Day was gone, Night covered sky,
Black over earth. When we came there,
To Brandon Walls, Where Red Shaw lay,
Hateful and sleeping, Unfriendly visit.
I wished to revenge, Quit fully
Who my father at Colefangs Valley,
Lying in ambush, Cruelly shot,

With life for life. . . .
There he died, Nor any came,
Fighters home, Nor wives shall go
Smiling to bed. They boast no more. (18)

Not only have Nower's men succeeded in killing Red Shaw, they have found his brother hiding in an outhouse. Nower orders killing at which the spy warns him: "You may look big, but we'll get you one day, Nower." At last Nower is satisfied by the killings. Left to himself he finds himself for the first time in a state of moral isolation. He soliloquizes:

Always the following wind of history
Of other's wisdom makes a buoyant air
Till we come suddenly on pockets where
Is nothing loud but us; where voices seem
Abrupt, untrained, competing with no lie
Our fathers shouted once. They taught us war
To scamper after darlings, to climb hills,
To emigrate from weakness, find ourselves
The easy conquerors of empty bays:
But never told us this, left each to learn,
Hear something of that soon-arriving day
When to gaze longer and delighted on
A face or idea be impossible. (19)

Nower expresses a strong yearning to get away from the system with its obnoxious pattern of strife, ambition resulting in empty fulfilment. He longs for an evolutionary past:

Could I have been some simpleton that lived
Before disaster sent his runners here;
Younger than worms, worms have too much to bear.
Yes, mineral were best: could I but see
These woods, these fields of green, this lively world
Sterile as moon. (20)

He wishes he were a mineral so that he need not make a choice. He is obviously dissatisfied with the tradition he has inherited from his class and wishes he were born before society reached the stage of corruption and disintegration.

The chorus appearing immediately after John's soliloquy presents the economic world of 1930:

> The spring unsettles sleeping partnerships,
> Foundries improve their casting process, shops,
> Open a further wing on credit till
> The winter. . . .
> War is declared there, here a treaty signed;
> Here a scum breaks up like a bomb, there troops
> Deploy like birds. But proudest into traps
> Have fallen. These gears which ran in oil for week
> By week, needing no look, now will not work;
> Those manors mortgaged twice to pay for love
> Go to another. (20)

In the second section, the chorus comments on man's condition:

> O how shall man live
> Whose thought is born, child of one farcical night,
> To find him old? The body warm but not
> By choice. . . .
> Outside on frozen soil lie armies killed
> Who seem familiar but they are cold. . . .
> Better where no one feels,
> The out-of-sight, buried too deep for shafts. (20)

In an obvious allusion to the millions of people killed in the First World War, the chorus seems to agree with Nower that the world is evil.

The scenes following the speeches of John Nower and the chorus take place in the sub-conscious of John Nower. He dreams a play-within-a-play. The inner drama of his own psyche begins with the important pivotal episode—the entry of Father Christmas.

The inner depths of Nower's mind are revealed. William Empson points out the use of surrealism in this episode while Cook traces its origins to the Mummers's and Folk Plays of medieval and probably earlier origin: "As the folk plays still held within their often broken forms the symbolic representation, of the basic forces and movements of nature, fertility, death, rebirth, seasonal change etc., so Auden, in his use of the folk-play material, suggests the basic drives at work at the centre of John's being, surviving as it were, from the early stages of his personal history."[9]

As in a Mummers's play, Father Christmas is the presenter in *Paid on Both Sides*. His prologue is brief. He thanks the spectators for coming and promises them a little surprise. Obviously employing the contradictions characteristic of the Mummers's play, he asks the audience to "tell . . . friends to come and bring the kiddies, but . . . remember to keep this a secret." (21) As Forrest E. Hazard suggests, "Auden used the name Father Christmas instead of one of the others probably to emphasize the spirit of brotherhood which the season should inspire. He chose the abrupt entrance for the presenter perhaps to suggest the abruptness of dreams. And he kept the prologue short evidently to concentrate on the body of the dream."[10]

In the traditional Mummers's play there is a physical combat between two chief protagonists but in Auden's play the action takes place in a court scene presided by Father Christmas. The spy who has been killed by Nower is being tried. Nower, himself the prosecutor, makes out a case for continuing the feud. The first witness, Bo, pleads for a change of heart and argues that the old way be given up. Po, the second witness, presents the opposite point of view. What Auden presents here is a discussion, not a combat.

After the courtroom scene, the Man-Woman, a relic of the Mummers's play, is presented. This figure derives, as Hazard says, "from the belief found in many religions that the dogs are bisexual."[11] Auden uses this androgynous figure to relate it to the theme of rebirth. As a symbol of life-force, it urges mankind to overcome regressive tendencies and work for psychic harmony and universal brotherhood. The speech of the Man-Woman, as F.W. Cook suggests, "is an ingenious projection of the closed world (of the psyche and society) in which John finds himself the result of Mother-fixation which gives to autoeroticism and other forms of sexual perversion."[12] John Nower's oedipal narcissicism is externalized in the Man-Woman speech and we know too well that Homer Lane's teachings, which Auden was probablv reading at the time of the composition of the *Paid on Both Sides* conditioned his thought. The desire for spiritual freedom, antagonism to parental authority are dramatized here.

In the Mummers's play a doctor is presented who boasts of his medical skill. The horseplay with the Doctor in *Paid on Both Sides* is after the Folk Plays, especially the extravagant wording of the tooth-extraction speech. The remarkable accomplishment of Auden in this part of the play is that he compressed the summoning of the doctor and the bargaining into four lines to maintain the rapid pace of the dream.

The doctor is brought in to cure the spy who has been shot by Nower. He cures the spy by extracting an enormous tooth from his body and exercising the ancestral curse: "This tooth was growing ninety-nine years before his great grandmother was born. If it hadn't been taken out today he would have died yesterday." (24) The spy gets up and the Accuser and Accused plant a tree. The lines, "Same time sharers of the same house,/We know not the builder nor the name of his son," indicate Nower and the spy are free from their ancestral past. They have come out victorious.

After the Father-Christmas fantasy episode, Nower wakes from the dream, calls for his horse and sets out to propose marriage to Anne Shaw. In his soliloquy, he discovered social and personal healing power of love. He likens his life to a city. Now he is "lighted and clean" but "made a slum" of his life before. Love has replaced "pride and indifference." The father Christmas passage, taking place in Nower's dream, is a warning against the world in which he lives. It offers Nower "moral guidance when the values of his feud-ridden social order prove inadequate. Using several metaphors, it urges him to abandon the worn out past, undergo the transitional privations attendant upon the change, and begin anew more in harmony with the life force."[13] Nower's soliloquy is a natural transition from the dream. The dream warning serves the purpose and now Nower contemplates inter-marriage with Anne as a way out of both feud and emotional sterility.

The chorus (27) following Nower's soliloquy is very important in that its meaning is immeasurable. It suggests that "To throw away the key and walk away," to be indifferent to the inherited feud, to emigrate (like Dick), to marry (like Nower and Anne) is to spoil the charade or the game. One should stay in the game and must respect the historical process.

While John Nower is planning to marry Anne Shaw, the feud continues. At least one on each side is killed. Nower's cure cannot affect the society he lives in. The neurosis involves entire society. The Announcer announces John's engagement to Anne. The two sides mix, "shake hands and cross over the stage to their opposite sides." (29). John and Anne try to undo the past and begin afresh. Anne knows that the state of feud has not ended. She therefore proposes emigration but John says, "you may be right, but we shall stay." His ambition is to rebuild and not escape, to defeat the dead and not flee. The murder of the spy has brought about a change in him but the same murder is remembered with undiminished intensity by his enemies. As Edward Mendelson observes: "There are two kinds of time in *Paid on Both Sides:* a personal time in which mutation is possible and the dead past can be barred from the living present, and a social time that changes, is never renewed, where habit rules unchanged."[14] It is the social time that triumphs in the play.

The final scene of the play, after the wedding party, returns to the opening condition of revenge and war. Seth is persuaded by his mother to kill John Nower: "Have you forgotten your brother's death . . . taken out and shot like a dog? It is a nice thing for me to hear people saying that I have a coward for a son. I am thankful your father is not here to see it."(33) John is killed and the feud continues. The Sophoclean chorus, equalling in beauty with earlier choruses, sums up the themes of the play:

> Though he believe it, no man is strong.
> He thinks to be called the fortunate,
> To bring home a wife, to live long.

But he is defeated; let the son
Sell the farm lest the mountain fall;
His mother and her mother won. (34)

Hynes remarks: "The theme of entropy, the old life running down, emerges . . . most movingly in the final speech of the play. . . . It is a somber ending, in the tone of classical tragedy: call no man fortunate who is not dead. Maturity is a long dying, death is a defeat; the mothers win, the son loses—which means . . . that continuity of life survives, but at the cost of individual life. In terms of the central theme of action, it is a dark reminder of the power of the enemy the past."[15]

It may be said that *Paid on Both Sides* is a dramatization of ideas embodied in the volumes of poetry that have appeared at the same time as the play. Auden's indictment of society wedded to illness by the forces of its fears, its immature sexuality, its eagerness to sidetrack energies, its inability to establish a vital relationship with Eros are all there. *Paid* derives its meaning against this context. The representatives of the old and new societies, their perpetual mutual denial and the consequent decadence form the landscape. The new is struggling to escape the old but freedom from the oppressive hold lies across the frontier: "The central metaphor vindicating new allegiances is that of disease: the old life is diseased, the new life represents health. The old life is arraigned because it lacks the power to cure itself: Health demands change and growth, it demands, precisely, evolution; and the old order has grown rigid."[16] The diseased legacy of the past is rendered in terms of a story. Auden seems to suggest that memory is death and man to overcome frustration and fatality and to regain health must break with forms of behaviour which are ruinous.

It may thus be seen that *Paid on Both Sides* "presents an image of the essential human condition: By saga-characters, as by Anglo-Saxon warriors or Greek epic heroes, warfare is regarded as man's normal condition and peace is an accidental breathing space. Man constantly faces insecurity and danger; all he can do is to accept his fate bravely."[17] Such an image of human condition on which this work is centred is but to be expected of a poet who was intent on creating an imaginative landscape predicated on ideas derived from Icelandic sagas characterized by a kind of sensibility laconic and unrelenting and of Anglo-Saxon poetry which Auden studied at Oxford:

> The saga world is a school-boy world, with its feuds, its practical jokes, its dark threats conveyed in puns and riddles and understatements: "I think this day will end unluckily for some; but chiefly for those who least expect harm." I once remarked to Auden that the atmosphere of Gisli the Outlaw very much reminded me of our school days. He was pleased with the idea: and, soon after this, he produced his first play: *Paid on Both Sides*, in which the two worlds are inextricably confused that it is impossible to say whether the characters are really epic heroes or only members of a school O.T.C.[18]

It was a landscape from which several distinguished contemporaries of Auden like Graham Greene, Christopher Isherwood had drawn their most significant settings. Auden's deliberate use of what could be called smart manner seems intended to diffuse the tension if any created by the "conflict" in the play, which is expressive of his uncompromising counter-romantic stance. Significantly, though evoking a kind of Aeschylean moral grandeur, the play seems charged with a peculiar school-boy atmosphere which proves helpful to the realization of the psychological distance within which his ironic reflectiveness would figure. Moreover, in this play Auden seems to be playing the role of a prophet of history sporting a school-boy's blazer which points to his characteristic way of perspectivizing man's engagement with life. The chorus in this play serves not only as the voice of collective opinion on the emerging action but also as a commonsensical measure for assessing the convulsive efforts of man to realize or to structure meaning out of the contingent world:

> Though he believe it, no man is strong.
> He thinks to be called the fortunate,

To bring home a wife, to live long.

But he is defeated; let the son
Sell the farm lest the mountain fall;
His mother and her mother won.

His fields are used up where the moles visit,
The contours worn flat; if there show
Passage for water he will miss it:

Give up his breath, his woman, his team;
No life to touch, though later there be
Big fruit, eagles above the stream. (34)

Though Auden's English critics consider the two phases of Auden's career occasioned by his migration to America in 1939 and identify with the English and American Audens as being distinct, the American critics are struck by the extraordinary cohesion that characterize his work as a whole. In this, Auden seems to have helped them by rejecting much of his early work and by refashioning what is left of it. It is therefore not surprising that the social, political, psychological and philosophical questions raised implicitly or explicitly in this play came to be elaborated upon or made use of in his later works although the patterns of emphasis marking them have undergone modifications. This play is undoubtedly emblematic of what could be designated as Audenesque psycho-aesthesis.

NOTES

1. William Empson, "A Note on Auden's *Paid on Both Sides*," *Experiment*, 7 (Spring 1931), pp. 60-61.
2. Samuel Hynes, *The Auden Generation* (London: The Bodley Head, 1970), p. 47.
3. *Loc. cit.*
4. *Ibid.*, pp. 47-48.

5. Quoted in Early Auden, p. 81.
6. *Loc. cit.*
7. *Paid on Both Sides* in *Collected Longer Poems* (London: Faber, 1968).
8. *A Reader's Guide to W.H. Auden* , p. 16.
9. F.W. Cook, "Primordial Auden," *Essays in Criticism*, 12 (October 1962), p. 407.
10. Forrest E. Hazard, "The Father Christmas Passage in *Paid on Both Sides*," *Modern Drama*, 12 (September 1969), p. 157.
11. *Ibid.*, p. 158.
12. F.W. Cook, p. 410.
13. F.E. Hazard, pp. 163-64.
14. *Early Auden*, p. 53.
15. Hynes, pp. 53-54.
16. Herbert S. Greenberg, *Quest for the Necessary: W.H. Auden and the Dilemma of Divided Consciousness* (Cambridge: Harvard University Press, 1968), p. 19.
17. Spears, *The Poetry of W.H. Auden: The Disenchanted Island*, p. 17.
18. Christopher Isherwood, "Some Notes on Auden's Early Poetry," *Auden*, ed. Monroe K. Spears, p. 11.

The Dog Beneath the Skin or *Where is Francis?*

The Dog Beneath the Skin or *Where is Francis?* (1935) has a special status in the Auden canon on account of its being the only work of his that brings out the image of Auden as a humane and witty man of letters with a pronounced aversion to *esprit de serieux* which tends to bloat up the writer's egotism and drives him to make Messianic claims—the image which has found favour with the largest section of readers. *Paid on Both Sides* and *The Dance of Death*, the early dramatic works with interesting flashes and plenty of evidence of real inventiveness have shown Auden's disposition to improvise devices from almost any source and to combine a variety of styles within a single work. They anticipate in this respect his next play *The Dog Beneath the Skin* which is ambitious in scope and shows a greater care in the craftsmanship. There is less of the obscurity of *Paid* and little of the difficulty of *The Dance* and presents fewer problems of interpretation.

The Dog Beneath the Skin is the third and final version of a play on which Auden worked for about three years in collaboration with Christopher Isherwood in respect of its first and third drafts. As all the three versions are available, it may be interesting to examine them from the standpoint of the evolution of a work of art. Rarely has a literary work undergone such radical changes in the process of being "finalized" as it were. Mardi Valgemae gives an elaborate account of the "genesis" and "the actual division of labour" in the making of *The Dog Beneath the Skin* after examining the documents which "shed considerable light on some of that dark terrain of joint authorship." Assuring that the joint authorship was in fact a "genuine collaboration," Valgemae concludes that "the credit for practically all the poetry in *The Dog Beneath the Skin* naturally goes to Auden, but much of its theatricality, especially many of the individual, fully dramatic episodes without which a play would collapse, must be credited to Isherwood."[1]

The first draft, *The Enemies of a Bishop, or, Die When I say When: A Morality in Four Acts* was written in 1932. "It concerned a White-slave ring, a group of escapees from a reformatory, and a lead-mine manager who seduces his assistant manager's wife with the help of the Devil. The theme of the play was the early-Auden faith in love and freedom. The Bishop, according to Isherwood, represented 'natural law,' and was modelled on Homer Lane, the heterodox psychiatrist, whom Auden admired at the time; his enemies were essentially the same as The Enemy in *The Orators*—all those who distort and repress life, love, and freedom."[2] It may be said following the major thrust of the plot that there are close affinities between *The Orators* and *The Enemies of a Bishop*. In the former, Auden tries to probe the sickness of the individual and that of society suggesting that repression and suppression left the individual a neurotic. The sickness is described by him as psychosomatic illness which can be cured by liberating the libido or sexual energy. Several poems in *The Orators* have this symptom-cure formula, the finest example being "Sir, No Man's Enemy."

The second version of *The Dog* called *The Chase* uses some of the components of *The Enemies of a Bishop*, but shifts the focus from love and freedom to class struggle: "There is a strike at the centre of the play, and capitalists who oppose it. There is also a character—one of the escaped prisoners from the first version—who appears disguised as a dog, and a quest for a missing heir. Like the previous version, *The Chase* is set entirely in England, but its themes are very different, concerned with economic and social history, rather than with psychic sickness and health. The mood of the play is the anti-capitalist, pro-working class mood of the early thirties, the years of greatest unemployment, of the first Hunger Marches, and of the collapse of the Labour Party. It is a play about domestic political and social issues, as an educated liberal young poet might see them."[3] The second draft speaks of

Auden's interest in Marxism. Like other thirties's poets, Auden too had his Marxist phase, but his Marxism largely centres round the philosophical formula, "freedom is the appreciation of necessity." If man has knowledge of causal connections between objects he will have the ability to control the external world. This theme is at the core of several early poems of Auden and the anti-capitalist stance is very much in the background and never comes centre stage.

The third version of the play, attempted in 1934 jointly by Auden and Isherwood and published in 1935, shows that much has been retained from the earlier versions: "it is patched and layered like a too-often-mended garment, and it is partly for that reason that it reads (and plays) more like a revue made up of satirical turns than a continuous dramatic statement. It includes, for example, "The Witnesses," which was originally a part of the allegorical poem that Auden wrote in 1932, and the Nineveh Hotel scene from *The Enemies of a Bishop*, and the Sermon from *The Chase*. There are passages of Lawrentian love, of psychological analysis, and of social concern for the poor and the distressed, and at various points satirical comments on patriotic rhetoric, anti-German hysteria, and class attitudes. In fact, one can find on one page or another virtually all the ideas that engaged Auden's imagination, and the imaginations of his generation, during the first half of the thirties. What remains constant through all the versions of the play, and all the laminations of the final text, is the intention that Auden announced when he called his first version 'A Morality': the point changes, but the motive does not."[4] It may be observed that the main difference between *The Dog* and its earlier version is that it is about Europe for which, it has been suggested, Isherwood is partly responsible. The scene in which Ostnian workers are executed by the King and the Queen's comforting words to the widows is based on Isherwood's personal knowledge. During his stay in Berlin, he had heard about Vienna Uprising and the cruel killings of workers. It is, therefore, reasonable to suppose that he must have pressed anti-fascist convictions upon his friend Auden who incorporated them in the final version of their collaborative work.

The Dog also differs from its earlier versions in its ending in that Francis is not murdered but is merely made to leave Pressan.

In the earlier versions Francis is murdered, and the journalists announce: "Nothing has happened."[5] This change seems to suggest that Auden and Isherwood were at times themselves in doubt about the final directions of their plays. A similar attempt was made by the collaborators in *On the Frontier*. In the Third Act of the latter play, an interlude presents readers of five different newspapers who give contradicting reports of the war followed by the despairing cries of Anna and Eric. In an earlier version "a revolutionary end followed the outbreak of war between the two states, the people seizing power."[6] In the final version "frustration is briefly substituted for the original 'straight' solution, producing an effect of bathos after the steadily increasing dramatic tension of what has preceded it."[7]

The Dog Beneath the Skin projects an unusual combination of issues—political, cultural, philosophical and existential—not all of which are explicit. If regarded as a political play, *The Dog Beneath the Skin* would appear to have remarkably succeeded in articulating the paranoid attitude to Germany in the English mind occasioned by the upsurge of Fascism in Germany. Auden offers in this regard an interesting contrast to E.M. Forster in his thematic treatment of Germany in *Howards End*.. While Forster remains a liberal humanist in projecting the German culture, Auden too seems committed to Marxist ideology to be able to view the German scene from a disinterested point of view. This may be attributed to Forster being drawn to the spirit of the place as it were and not to its people or their culture which explains his view of German imperialism as "the imperialism of the air" or of Germans as the countrymen of Hegel and Kant, not as they would appear in the present. But Auden reacted differently to Germany since he was typically English in his abhorrence of totalitarianism or Authoritarianism in which his Marxist leanings seemed to have had a decisive say.

The play *The Dog Beneath the Skin* or *Where is Francis?* is concerned with an unusual quest—that of Alan Norman who goes in search of the heir of Pressan Ambo, Francis. The play details the seeming adventures of the hero as he journeys from place to place seeking the missing heir and in the process being affected by them in the way Strether in Henry James's *Ambassadors* is "converted" or transformed. But the comparison between the two cannot be pressed far because Strether has none of the innocence that defines Alan's personality which makes all the difference to the evaluation of Alan's experiences. The story implied in *The Dog Beneath the Skin* may be termed as initiation story only through the exercise of critical ingenuity since Alan's encountering an experience though suggestive of initiation rites is Blakean in conception. This is the reason why Alan "conversion" as it were is more existential than experiential in that he comes to evaluate life in terms which regard existence as a principle rather than a context. The varied experiences which he has in the course of his travels spell different aspects of man's engagement with life to which he is a witness. It is significant that the striking experiences which Alan has in different contexts of being seem intended as focal points in the narrative design contributing to the hermeneutic chemistry which Auden attempts in this play. It is but to be expected that the action of the play flow through the mind of Alan rather than the events punctuating his quest—an action that turns Alan's innocence into an exasperated consciousness of the betrayal of the possibilities of the human personality. The discovery that brings the quest to an abrupt end, that of Francis being "the True Son, the Hero's Friend, the clear-sighted, intelligent, and honourable Leader," though startling has the effect of turning the whole play into a fantasia expressive of an investigation of the nature of truth which is as central an issue in the action as in the so-called business of rule or government.

Ostnia and Westland, which are symbolic of decadent monarchy and fascist dictatorship respectively, appear for the first time in *The Dog Beneath the Skin*. They will appear again in *On the Frontier*. As politico-poetic plays, these two are complementary as each illuminates and reinforces the subject of the other. In *The Ascent of F6* also, there are two countries but in place of Ostnia and Westland, there are British Sudoland and Ostnian Sudoland. The plays present two types of governments and suggest the inadequacies inherent in each. There is nothing to choose between them. If in one country the power is concentrated in a few individuals, in the other country the power is wielded by one individual. The dangers of colonialism, monarchism and fascism are some of the themes of the play.

The chorus is an important element of this play. It speaks more lines than any character and is given the best lines in the play. It is a choric commentator that leads the spectators along the course of the action. Besides the chorus there are Semi-Chorus I and Semi-Chorus II, appearing singly or in succession. The criticism that the chorus and the action of the play move in opposite directions, that there is no co-ordination between them, needs to be corrected. Julian Symons remarks that "the picture of life and humanity created in the choruses was one thing, and the action of the play quite another... that the choruses and the action seemed to belong to different plays."[9] Duchene, identifying the techniques of the modern musical comedy and pre-medieval folk play in *The Dog Beneath the Skin,* says: "In the choruses Auden seemed to be writing for his muse, in the action writing down to his 'pre-medieval' audience. As there was far more action than choruses, the impression which sticks in the memory is of a superlative under-graduate romp and of the coming of age of Auden's musical-hall style, lithe, brilliant and shallow."[10] A more sympathetic view takes into consideration the coalescing of morality and musical comedies by Auden. Since the play begins and ends with a critical and satirical survey of the delusions, sins, follies, and psychoses of post-war Europe, its design permits the widest possible variety in styles. "Accordingly there is everything from doggerel to the stately measures of the choruses. The tendency of the modern poet to range freely among all possibilities, to subject old styles to new purposes, so that a jazz song takes on serious overtones and a Caroline Lyric emerges with an unexpected ironic edge, is here illustrated to the full. What gives direction to all this variety is the choruses, which appear almost invariably before each scene. Written for the most part in a uniform style and with uniform seriousness and dignity of tone, the choruses establish the themes which the episodes treat with a diversity of devices."[11]

The play opens on Pressan Ambo, an English village. The scene, the garden of the Vicarage, "suggests the setting of a pre-war musical comedy."[12] (17) There are villagers of all classes on the stage and each of them addresses the audience as they pass along the footlights. Unlike the conventional play wherein the opening expository scene introduces major characters and the theme or themes of the play, the opening scene of this play doesn't formally present the plot. The "characters," the Vicar, the General and his wife, introduce themselves. They claim themselves to be the custodians of Pressan Ambo. The Vicar sounds simple and innocuous: "I labour to expound the truth/To train the tender plant of Youth/And guard the moral order." (17) General Hotham, who won fame at Tatra Lakes and took the Spanish Lion, now has made Pressan his home, and "rule my house like a brigade/With discipline of iron." (17) The General's wife, who keeps the General's heart, does her utmost to advance "In India, Russia, Finland, France/The just and English glory." (18) The Princess Iris Crew, complacent and adolescent, tells the spectators that she is the prize at village dances and has now come to take their glances. The audiences are not supposed to take the utterances of the above for truth. The picture is completed by the chorus, which breaks the bubble. For example, the chorus comments on General's wife: "With subtle will and female smile, /With speech and vote she will promote/The just and English glory." (18)

After the brief introductory verses are spoken, the Vicar now speaks about the purposes for which the people have met. In a ballad-like manner, the verse address to the spectators recalls the story of Crewes. Sir Francis Crew, son and heir to Sir Bingham Crew, quarrelled with his father on a trivial matter, "packed and ran away/Leaving behind him no address," (22) ten years ago. Sir Bingham Crew died two years after, heart-broken and ill and left these clauses in his will:

> Each year, his village in turn
> Should choose by lottery a man
> To find Sir Francis if he can:
> Further, he promised half his land,
> And Iris his daughter adds her hand
> In marriage to the lucky one
> Who comes home with his only son. (23)

It is Pressan's turn to choose a person by lottery now. A villager sings expressing the sense of loss felt by the community:

> Without his face we don't know what to do,
> We are undone
> He was a beauty with a sense of duty too,
> He was our brother and our son.
> His wit, his charm, his strength, his manliness, his modesty and his virtue
> Were we to tell, your contrast, well, with him would hurt you. (24)

The yearning for the missing prince appears to be genuine as the above sentiments testify. One wonders whether the villager is contrasting the wit, virtue and modesty of the Prince with those who are running the government or whether he is contrasting the Prince's great qualities of head and heart with the others in the country. Since the common men are not expected to be ideal and heroic, one may reasonably conclude that the villager is contrasting the Prince with the General and his cohorts.

Princess Iris Crew swears to be the wedded wife of the person who brings back her brother. The Curate reads out the names of those who are unmarried and over twenty-five. Alan Norman is chosen and he assures the Vicar to cross any border in sand or snow, "Though people and customs both be hateful, /When mind and members go opposite way." (25) As each one prepares to bid farewell to Alan Norman, a dog comes over there, disregards the importunities of the Vicar and the General "with an almost human contempt" and reaches Alan, who begins calling it Francis and decides to take it along his quest.

The next scene describes the beginning of the quest for the missing heir. Alan Norman boards a channel steamer and meets with two Journalists. The latter notice Alan with his dog and are surprised to find the dog drinking whisky. Alan enquires the barman of the channel steamer if he has seen Francis and not able to describe him and finding the photograph he carries which was taken when Francis was six months old unhelpful, he now wants to go to Ostnia to see if Francis is there. The second Journalist, who knows Ostnia like the inside of his hat, offers the following account:

> Pretty little country, Ostnia. Biggest national debt and lowest birth-rate in Europe. Half the budget goes into frontier forts, which are no more use than a headache because the contractor's a crook. The railways are of so old they aren't safe, the mines are mostly flooded and the factories do nothing but catch fire. The Commander-in-Chief is not better than a bandit: He makes all the big stores pay for protection. The Archbishop spends his time copying naval plans for the Westland Intelligence Bureau. And meanwhile, the peasants die of typhus. . . . it's God's own land. (38-39)

The Ostnia that is described continues into the other plays. It represents the corruption, inhumanity and tyranny that were common traits in the European dictatorial states between the two World Wars.

As Alan, the Dog, and the Journalists land in the Ostnian capital, they find the whole city mourning. They are told that there has been a revolt against the King and the criminals are being executed that day. They meet the King and Queen of Ostnia who most impudently talk about executions and worse still direct them to the Red Light District to find Alan. The bitterly ironic attitude towards rulers is apparent in the presentation of the ruthless attitude which the King, nobility, and clergy hold toward the killings. The scene, it has been suggested, was inspired by 1934 Civil War in Austria.[13] In the Red Light District, Alan and the Journalists are accosted by proprietors of cafes who tempt them with girls and boys of every shape and size. Alan meets Sorbo Lamb, who had come earlier on a similar mission like his, and realizes that the latter had fallen a victim to the flesh trade. Alan persuades him to get away from this rot but Sorbo Lamb says:

> Don't you see these chains? My punishment and my reward. The light of your world would dazzle me and its noises offend my ears. Fools! How could you possibly appreciate my

exquisite pleasures? Sometimes I lie quite still for days together, contemplating the flame of a candle or the oscillating shadow of a lamp. What revelations, what bottomless despairs! Please leave me alone. (62)

From the Ostnian capital, Alan moves on to Westland. Significantly he lands himself in a lunatic asylum, a metaphor for Westland. There is confusion worse confounded. The men and women are guided by "our Leader," a man with a loud-speaker for a face. The portrayal of the man with a loud-speaker for a face has been described as "an effective stroke of dramatic imagination."[14] The women are treated like hens and if they "don't lay properly we shall be fattened for the Christmas Market." On their part, the women "never wanted to be independent." As the lunatics begin quarrelling among themselves over a trivial matter, the Leader's voice is heard from the loud-speaker. His speech, carefully worded, the tone well-modulated, is typical of a fascist leader's. It begins by praising the land and her people and then directs people to the enemy:

> Not two hundred miles from where I stand, there is a Nation: trained to arms from infancy, schooled in military obedience and precision, saluting even in the cradle, splendidly equipped with every invention of modern science, able, resolute, taught to regard the individual as nothing and the State as all, scorning treaties as mere scraps of paper to be rent asunder when the interests of the State demand. My mind's eye saw the long silent grey ranks. I heard the shouting of the captains, the brazen call of the trumpet and the pawing of the chargers. And a voice said: Woe, woe to the unprepared: For their inheritance shall be taken away and their home be left desolate! (71)

It is ironical that whatever is attributed to the enemy country is more true of his (Leader's) own country. The Leader warns people of war and its consequences. Even insignificant things like a "piece of paper left by a picnic party which has inadvertently strayed over the frontier, a rash word in a letter about the superiority of Westland beer or a humorous sketch in a revue misunderstood'' can cause war. Destruction might come like a thief. Some of the terrifying results of war are on innocent babes, aged parents and school-going children. The Leader goes a little further and says that the ''flame once lit would spread into a universal conflagration. . . . Within a week our civilization, all that our statesmen and thinkers, our poets and musicians, have travailed for down the ages of history, would die a smoking ruin!'' (72-73) The Leader now exhorts people to be prepared for the leadership of the world by enforcing peace, build ''an air force of such magnitude that any enemy, however ferocious, will think twice before daring to strike,'' make sacrifices and live worthy of their responsibilities. The Leader's speech has the desired effect on the lunatics. There is tremendous enthusiasm among them. They consider every stranger, he be a Jew or a Marxist, a traitor. In that mood of hysterical frenzy, they tie up Alan, who strays into their room, calling him rumour-monger, non-Aryan, separatist grumbler etc. The journalists rescue Alan from them.

From the Westland lunatic asylum, Alan and the Journalists move on and board a train. While they talk about political scandals of all kinds, they see a Financier and Alan is persuaded to blackmail him. The Financier, on being identified, turns deadly pale but soon recovers his composure and offers a handsome amount in compensation for not exposing his scandals like forging the report on the diamond mines on Tuesday Island, staging the fake attempt on the Prince of the Hellespont in order to corner the rubber market, and getting the men murdered who were going to show up the Bishop of Pluvium. The Financier offers to take Alan as his secretary on ten thousand pounds and, on hearing that Alan is on a different mission, directs him to Paradise Park.

In this interesting encounter between Alan and the Financier, we gain an insight into the lot of the capitalists. They are forgers, murderers, and exploiters. They bribe the journalists who threaten to expose their scandals, and buy wholesale newspaper concerns. The Financier's attitude to poets is that ''most of them are moral degenerates or Bolsheviks, or both. The scum of the earth.'' (87) We also see the pathetic side of the Financier whose life is the story of ambition coupled with hard work. The Financier says:

I've founded hospitals and rest-homes,
  Subscribed to public funds,
Promoted schemes for planning Best Homes
  And built a school for nuns.
I've studied all the Italian Masters,
  I've tried to read French books,
But all my efforts seem disasters:
  I only get such nasty looks. (88)

This is the positive side of the Financier, of the capitalists. They try to compose their acts of exploitation by founding hospitals and by subscribing to public funds. The Financier emotionally speaks: "None of them like me. Wherever I go I see it. I can't so much as get a really friendly smile out of a railway porter, though, Heaven knows I tip them enough." (87) Subsequently we understand that he is disliked by his only son and his wife.

Alan Norman and the Dog reach the gardens of Paradise Park "where most wasters and cranks land up sooner or later" (89-90) while the journalists follow the Financier. In one of the trees sits the Poet. In the other are two Lovers. Asked if he has seen Sir Francis, the Poet tapping his forehead says everything is there. He seems to think that he is the centre of the world and to believe that the external world will disappear if he closes his eyes. The Poet feels alienated from the world and its people and he refuses to communicate to them. He prefers to live in a world of fantasy, a characteristic of artists as has been pointed out by Freud. Alan then meets the Lovers who are "going to be lovers all our life:/Two as one and one as two." This is followed by his meeting with invalids of all kinds.

Later Alan finds himself, also in the Paradise Park, in the operating theatre peopled by patients, students and the Surgeon. In this farcical scene, we find the indifference, incompetence and carelessness of the men of medical profession. While a certain operation is in progress, lights go off and instead of adrenalin the nurse gives hydrochloric acid and the patient dies. He is no other than Chimp Eagle, Alan's predecessor in the quest, who forgot "My choice and lot."

The Third Act presents some of the hateful, hideous, ugly, barbarous attributes of modern civilization. It is a civilization devoid of morals, spiritual values and is utterly indecent and vulgar. The authors seem to suggest that modern civilization has no need for culture. They view the fate of culture with deep pessimism. In the stage direction to Scene ii, the playwrights say: "The entire setting of this scene should convey an impression of brutal, noisy vulgarity and tasteless extravagance." (124) The entire scene is a sad comment on the contemporary society whose values have reached rock bottom and whose members inhabit the waste land.

Alan and the two Journalists, who have returned after a brief separation, are now at Nineveh Hotel. The cabaret dancer, Madame Bubbi, in her performance, which is attended by a large gathering, displays her voluptuous charms and along with other call girls submits herself to "masculine inspection." The stage direction reads: "All that is mechanical, shallow, silly, hideous and unbearably tragic in the antics of a modern cabaret chorus should be expressed here in its most exaggerated form. Crude lighting. Rowdy music." (126) The expressionistically distorted cabaret scene was "suggested" by Bertolt Brecht's *Rise and Fall of the City of Mahagonny*.[15]

Destructive Desmond episode,[16] also in Nineveh Hotel, following Madame Bubbi's cabaret performance, presents yet another aspect of modern man's total disregard for values, values which have been held dear and cherished for centuries. Arts and literatures of the past have become worthless. Modern man delights in burning up treasures which have been handed down to him. He not only delights himself but makes a public celebration of his cult and cheers many. One such person is Destructive Desmond. There is deafening applause once his appearance is announced. His personal appearance is as clumsy as his mind. A "stocky, middle-aged man, with an inflamed, pugnacious face and very hairy knees," he "is dressed as a school-boy, with ink-stains on his cheeks, a crumpled eton collar, a striped cap, broken bootlaces, dishevelled stockings and shorts." (128) He had earned notoriety by burning up an entire "first folio Shakespeare, page by page." Rupert Doone cut out this scene when he produced the play in January 1936.

As he comes on to the stage, he asks for "a nice old poetry-book." The audience burst into laughter since they know why he has asked for it. Then Destructive Desmond uncovers two paintings—one Rembrandt's valued at sixty thousand pounds "something unique . . . a work of genius . . . which can't be replaced. . . . Priceless," the other "a completely tasteless piece of third-rate Victorian landscape painting." He takes out a knife to slash the Rembrandt canvas. An Art Expert among audience protests "against this disgraceful exhibition" but Desmond slashes the canvas to pieces respecting the majority opinion. Louis MacNeice presents a similar scene to show modern man's contemptuous attitude toward culture in *Out of the Picture* (1937).

This scene is followed by the presentation of Miss Lou Vipond "The star of whom the world is fond!" The diners at the Nineveh Hotel jump up and rush towards her. Alan is one of the first. The Journalists dissuade him from the attempt but in vain. The Dog also tries to prevent him but Alan kicks it aside and goes to Miss Lou Vipond. His protestations of love are similar to that of the lovers in "As I walked out one Evening": "I would give the Netherlands with all their canals,/The earth of the Ukraine, The Niagara Falls,/The Eiffel Tower also and the Dome of St. Paul's." (141) He will ensure her loyalty by hunting "the enormous whale in the Arctic Lowlands,/I would count all the starlings in the British Islands,/I would run through fighting Europe in absolute silence." (142) Alan tears up Iris's picture to pieces saying he cares only for Vipond's beauty and embraces the shop-window dummy.

At this moment in the play, the audience are in for a great surprise. As Alan Norman sleeps with the dummy in the dark room, the dog's voice is heard in the corridor and after sometime Francis Crew emerges out of the dog's skin and goes out. It is ironical that Alan is not able to know the person who has always been with him. Alan is disturbed by the Hotel Manager and is given a bill for fifteen hundred pounds. He is amazed at it and pleads with Vipond to help him out of the awkward situation. There is no reason for his entreaties. When the Manager goes out to bring police, Alan discovers to his pleasant surprise that Francis has been hiding in the skin. Now Alan and Francis exchange places and escape from the Hotel.

The last scene of the play, like the opening scene, takes the audience to Pressan Ambo. The action, which was set in motion in Pressan, ends where it began. The quester, who was given a warm farewell, has come back in great success. But Pressan, more precisely the Garden of the Vicarage, has lost its innocence. It has forgotten the missing heir and the quester. It does not look forward to either of them. Alan, Francis, still in disguise, and the two Journalists arrive in Pressan which wears a festive look. From the Curate they gather that

> The Lads of Pressan is a Boy's Brigade founded by the Vicar and General Hotham. Miss Iris Crew is Patroness and Mrs Hotham Honorary Colonel-in-chief. The uniforms have been designed by the Vicar. Today, the Brigade is to have its first inspection by General and Mrs. Hotham. The Vicar will preach a sermon on Bolshevism and the Devil. And Miss Iris Crew will present the Standard, which will then be blessed by the Vicar. (160)

As for the objects of this Brigade "Standing outside all political parties and factions, for Church, King and State, against communism, terrorism, pacifism and other forms of international anarchy, to protect Religion and succour England in times of national crisis." (160)

The Vicar's long speech is, in a nutshell, a justification of monarchy and a gloss on the Divine Theory of Kingship. He refers to the Biblical myth of Adam unparadised and the original sin. In spite of Gabriel and Michael all was irrevocably lost. The "wonderful creature" Satan, "altered for ever and for the worse, (he) went out to corrupt others, to form his notorious and unfamous societies" In the heavenly war between God and bad angels, the latter fell like water into "the fosse of Hell." The Vicar, after narrating these events, warns people of Pressan that the danger is not over yet: "The scene of operations was transferred to another front, to us. Impotent to attack Him directly, the defeated sought to strike at God through

His creatures, to wound, where it was most tender." (165) To offset this attack, God set over the people "a kindly strictness, appointed His authorities, severe but just, a kind of martial law. He gave them power to govern in His name and access to His presence in their prayers, to make their reports and ask for help and guidance, that through them the people might leave His primary will." (166) In the name of God the Vicar is seeking to legitimize the martial law administered in Pressan. Disapproving the various political movements in the cause of freedom, the various political ideologies that address man "you are God," the Vicar conjures up visions of the world "if this lunacy with its grim fanatic theories were to spread over the civilized globe":

> No family love. Sons would inform against fathers, cheerfully send them to the execution cellars. Mothers send their daughters to the mines. No romance. Even the peasant must beget that standard child under laboratory conditions. Motherhood would be by licence. Truth and beauty would be proscribed as dangerously obstructive. To be beautiful would be treason against the State, Thought a sabotage deadly to the thinker. No books, no art, no music. A year of this, I say, and even the grass would cease to grow, flowers would not risk appearance, heifers would not dare to calve. (167)

Dismissing the enemies's boasts as vain and their strength as feeble, the Vicar exhorts the people to take swift decisions, have keen senses and constant will. He ends his long discourse in mock humility and with a prayer to God so that his people be admitted to the blessed country where the saints move happily.

At this point in the play Mildred Luce, whom audience have seen in the opening scene of the play and whose two sons have been shot by a German sniper, comes out of the crowd of villagers and warns the Lads of Pressan against the war-mongers, the Vicar and the General. Visibly annoyed at this, Mrs. Hotham takes away Mildred Luce from the place. The General fights hard to direct people on whom Mildred Luce's speech "has made the most painful impression" by complimenting the Lads of Pressan on "the excellent turn out'' and by announcing the gift of ''the Honeypot Hall Estate to the Lads of Pressan, as barracks, parade-ground and playing-fields'' and the marriage of Miss Iris Crew, with an armaments manufacturer. Now Alan rises to announce himself and Francis at which Iris swoons.

Francis begins to tell the people all that he has done since his life as a dog had begun. He has had a dog's-eye view of all:

> I was fascinated and horrified by you all. I thought such obscene, cruel, hypocritical, mean, vulgar creatures had never existed before in the history of the planet.... As a dog, I learnt with what a mixture of fear, bullying, and condescending kindness you treat those whom you consider your inferiors, but on whom you are dependent for your pleasures. It's an awful shock to start seeing people from underneath. (173)

After assuring the assembly that he has not come back to claim his lawful rights, he tells them that they are what he imagined they would be. Most of them will die without ever knowing what their leaders are really fighting for or even that they are fighting at all. Their choice is not his. With this Francis leaves, followed by Alan and a few recruits. The play ends with the chorus's final exhortation to choose.

In the revised version for the production in 1936, Auden cut off Francis's abandonment of Pressan and also the reference to ''the army of the other side.'' Francis now becomes an instructor in history and choice. Though there is a correspondence between Francis's opening speech in the 1935 and 1936 versions, the conclusion now is different:

> I don't hate you any more. You are significant but not in the way I used to imagine. You are not the extraordinary monsters I thought. You are not individually important. You are just units in an immense army; and most of you would probably die without knowing either what your leaders are really fighting for or even what you are fighting for all. . . . That ignorance at least I can do something to remove. I can't dictate

to you what to do and I don't want to either. I can only try to show you what you are doing and so force you to choose. For choice is what you are all afraid of.[17]

After Francis's challenge to the people of Pressan to elect a new life, he is made to die at the hands of Mildred Luce: "In this 1936 version Francis's death is the disaster the chorus urges us not to repeat in our lives, and the conclusion of the action is now consistent with the hortatory interludes."[18]

Cast in the mould of the fairy tale, approximating to the allegorical and symbolic, employing the conventions of musical comedy and revue, *The Dog Beneath the Skin* contains popular songs, prose parody, didactic choruses, lyrical skeltonics, doggerel. The fairy tale mode is exploited to take in varied themes like communism, fascism and Freudism. In spite of the co-existence of amalgam of beliefs, the play " is so candidly unpretentious as a whole that, like all 'light' literature, it makes a cunning claim for serious attention."[19] For I.M. Parsons, the play is "a shoddy affair, a half-baked little satire," "the dreariest, the flattest and the stalest"[20]; for Fuller the play "struck a happy balance between suggestive symbolism and myth, and direct caricature and propaganda: between doggerel, knockabout and pastiche, and some of Auden's finest lyrical and analytic poetry"[21]; for Derek Verschoyle the choruses, the dialogue, the prose scenes bear the mark of "a genuine dramatic talent."[22]

The Dog Beneath the Skin contains Brechtian dramatic conventions."[23] Auden himself admitted that he was influenced by Brecht's *Hauspostille* poems, *Three Penny Opera* (1928) and *Mahagonny* (1929). He collaborated with Brecht in adapting *The Duchess of Malfi* and translated Brecht's *The Seven Deadly Sins*. Brecht's theory of "epic theatre" sought to destroy dramatic illusion by presenting a curved course of episode and to make the spectators think. In *The Dog Beneath the Skin*, the hero's quest takes him to places and people of all kinds and his movements are punctuated by choral songs which align the play to musical comedy rather than to the conventional play. The political satire in the play is largely influenced by Brecht.

The Dog Beneath the Skin also adapts motion-picture modes oı narration. Auden's fondness for montage sequence in poetry has been noted already. In the composition of poetry, the Russian cinema of Pudovkin and Eisenstein helped him in the evocation of socio-political atmosphere by the assemblage of disparate yet relevantly selected shots—by montage. One can see the cinematic evocation of the full range of England's landscape with examples of every kind of place an audience might recognize as it owes in *The Dog Beneath the Skin*. Like Thomas Hardy in *The Dynasts*, Auden gives a panoramic view of Europe in this play. The play, indeed, is an amalgam of styles, themes and philosophical formula-table facts which is what makes it at once highly entertaining and illuminating.

NOTES

1. Mardi Valgemae, "Auden's Collaboration with Isherwood on *The Dog Beneath the Skin*," *Huntington Library Quarterly*, 31, 4 (1968), p. 373.
2. Samuel Hynes, p. 182
3. *Loc. cit.*
4. *Ibid.*, pp. 182-83.
5. Alan Wilde, *Christopher Isherwood* (New York: Twayne, 1971), p. 81.
6. John Lehman, *New Writing in England*, quoted in Alan Wilde, p. 81.
7. Alan Wilde, p. 81.
8. Barbara Everett, *Auden* (London: Oliver and Boyd, 1964), p. 54.
9. Julian Symons, pp. 79-80.
10. Francois Duchene, p. 75.
11. Moody E. Prior, *The Language of Tragedy* (Bloomington: Indiana University Press, 1950), p. 368.
12. *The Dog Beneath the Skin* (London: Faber, 1935).
13. Mardi Valgemae, p. 378.
14. Philip Blair Rice, "Toward a Poetic Drama," *Nation* (27 November 1935), p. 626.
15. Mardi Valgemae, "Auden's Collaboration with Isherwood on *The Dog Beneath the Skin*," p. 377.

16. While I.M. Parsons describes the scene as "clumsily ineffectual" and "untrue to life" ("Poetry, Drama and Satire," *Spectator* (28 June 1935), p. 1112) several other critics commented on the effectiveness of the episode. For example, Kenneth Allott, "Auden in the Theatre," *New Verse* (November 1937), p. 20; Richard Hoggart, *Auden: An Introductory Essay*, p. 77; Raymond Williams, *Drama from Ibsen to Eliot* (London: Chatto and Windus, 1952), p. 250; and Julian Symons, *The Thirties: A Dream Revolved* (London: Faber, 1960), p. 83.
17. Quoted in Edward Mendelson, *Early Auden* (London: Faber, 1981), p. 278.
18. *Ibid.*, p. 279.
19. Barbara Everett, p. 55.
20. Quoted in Charles Osborne, *W.H. Auden: The Life of a Poet* (London: Macmillan, 1982), p. 113.
21. John Fuller, *A Reader's Guide to W.H. Auden*, p. 79.
22. Quoted in Charles Osborne, p. 114.
23. The influence of Brecht on Auden has been discussed by Richard Hoggart, *Auden: An Introductory Essay*, pp. 73-74; Joseph Warren Beach, *The Making of the Auden Canon*, p. 148; Spears, *The Poetry of W.H. Auden*, pp. 90-92; John G. Blair, *The Poetic Art of W.H. Auden* (Princeton: Princeton University Press, 1965), pp. 17-18; Frederick Buell, *W.H. Auden as a Social Poet* (New York: Cornell University Press, 1973), p. 90.

The Ascent of F6: A Tragedy in Two Acts

The Ascent of F6 (1936), the second of the plays marking the collaboration between W.H. Auden and Christopher Isherwood, is remarkable in that it projects an intersection of the apocalyptic and contemporary time which is what makes it modernist in character. The play is charged with a sense of the ominousness which is characteristic of the time in which it came to be written—a time which witnessed a gathering of a storm as it were.[1] But the play owes its significance less to its topicality than to the profundity of the questions dealt with by it—questions such as those related to man's ascent up the ladder of dubieties, confusions, contradictions, anomalies marking his existence in the hope that it would turn out to be Jacob's Ladder. This does not mean that the quester hero of this play Michael Ransom is in search of any mystical apprehension of Reality nor is he interested in realizing what might be called "luminous humanism." There is, however, a suggestion of the hero being identifiable with Sisyphus although the myth of Sisyphus is not worked into the texture of the play. The play dramatizes man's struggle to find subjective answer to metaphysical questions stemming from his apprehension of his complex fate with which he seeks in Auden's formulation an "aesthetic truce" rather than anything proposed by religious mysticism.

The Ascent of F6 significantly centres on the ascent of a "Haunted Mountain" called F6 which might be likened to the one below, the highest heaven—the seventh. This implies a kind of recognition of man's incapacity as it were to scale the highest possible only through the achievement of Dantean Unity of Being which would mean to witness the spiritual truth and thus become daimonic. The rivalries of two nations to scale the Haunted Mountain is only expressive of the so-called public theme—the theme of nations preparing for war. Intertwined with it is the more important theme—the private one which is spelt out by the career of Michael Forsyth Ransom. The "fact" that a great scholar and mountaineer Ransom undertakes the hazardous attempt of climbing up the mountain impelled not by any idealistic aspiration but by a desire to please his mother is suggestive of the theme being concerned with the question of self-actualization or self-definition occasioned by Oedipal complex. In this respect, Ransom's career is reminiscent of the hero's in Shakespeare's *Coriolanus* although they are differently directed and atomized. Ransom's adventurous journey along the steep surface is as heart-breaking as that of Sisyphus and relates to what is converted by the Jungian Rite de passage. The play brings out the different phases marking his growth in self-awareness needed for achieving a breakthrough to a new identity structure. Significantly, the original impelling force, that of his Oedipal obsession which has driven him to the undertaking of this venture, seems not only unavailing as the journey progresses but singularly ineffete. The implication is that Ransom, symbolizing contemporary man, is assailed by a multiplicity of forces related as much to the congeries in his inner being as to the "displacements" caused by the outer world of his being. Ransom's reading of Canto XXVI of Dante's "Inferno" with which the play opens is suggestive of his seeking possible roles like that of Ulysses to realize a viable pattern for his quest of truth. Ransom's response to Ulysses's quest is not only radical but also revealing of the complexion of his soul which militates against the investing of Ulysses with any aura, spiritual or otherwise. In suggesting, as Ransom does, that it is not "Virtue and Knowledge" that Ulysses was in quest of but power is to strip the truth about Ulysses of its veil of poetry and to confront what is characteristic of human history:

> Ransom (reads): "O brothers!" I said, "who through a hundred thousand dangers have reached the West, deny not, to the brief vigil of your sense that remains, experience of the unpeopled world behind the Sun. Consider your origin: Ye were not formed to live like brutes, but to follow virtue and

knowledge." (Putting down the Book.) Virtue and Knowledge! One can picture Ulysses' audience: a crook speaking to crooks. Seedy adventurers, of whose expensive education nothing remained but a few grammatical tags and certain gestures of the head; refugees from the consequences of vice or eccentric and conceited opinions; natural murderers whom a peaceful winter had reduced to palsied wrecks; the ugly and cowardly who foresaw in a virgin land an era of unlimited and effortless indulgence; teachers without pupils, tormentors without victims, parasites without hosts, lunatic missionaries, orphans. (13)[2]

It is ironic that while rejecting a mythical Ulysses, Ransom actually casts himself in the role of the modern Ulysses driven by the same impulse to illumination needed for his imaginary metaphysical self-sufficiency. While scorning the author of the above lines, Ransom, in his self-deluding hubris, fails to recognize his own features in Dante's account of Ulysses, the great adventurer, who destroyed himself and his following. He does not realize his condemnation of Dante as a condemnation of himself. He fails also to recognize that it is he, not Dante, who seeks power; that it is he, not Dante, who sees the world as a formless chaos awaiting a redeemer who might give it order.

Christopher Isherwood, Auden's collaborator of the play, explained the story in terms of either T.E. Lawrence or contemporary dictators. Since mountaineering was considered a romantic enterprise, the collaborators represent it in the character of Michael Ransom. In the years between the wars, the British sent several groups of climbers to Everest and the Alps. These adventurers were given wide coverage and publicity in mass media. Even intellectuals considered mountain-climbing a heroic activity. Michael Roberts and his wife Janet Adam Smith, I.A. Richards and his wife were serious climbers. Most important of all, Auden's brother and Spender's cousin were in Eric Shipton's expedition. It is but natural that climber-hero appears in the thirties' literature. In fact, the climber became a metaphor for courage. Michael Roberts compares Auden's poetic courage to Irvine and Mallory on Everest. While

Auden and Isherwood were finalizing their play, a British and American expedition was scaling Nanda Devi, a Himalayan peak. The action of *F6* is similar to that of Nanda Devi climb, even in details. The press coverage of the expedition and the news broadcasting in the play are nearly the same. The play had a topical interest for these reasons.

Whether or not Michael Ransom is modelled after T.E. Lawrence as Isherwood admits, and whether or not he represents Hitler and other dictators, the fact remains that the analogies cease after the initial scenes of the play. The play not merely narrates the hero's adventures on his way upto F6, it points out his peculiar temptations, temptations which are not easily overcome. The latter half of the play, from the time when Ransom meets the Abbot on the mountain, deals with man's perennial problems in life. The "Truly Strong Man" that he promises to be at the beginning of the play, Ransom dismissing Ulysses and Dante in one breath at the Summit of the Pillar Rock pronounces himself pure in heart, and clean in his motives: "let me receive such vigour and the impassive embraces of this sullen rock afford, from which no mastery can elicit a gratifying response, nor defeat sighs capable of despairing misinterpretation. Here is no knowledge, no communication, no possession; nothing that a bishop could justify, a stockbroker purchase or an elderly scientist devote years to explaining—only the voluntary homage paid by the living to the unqualified and dangerous dead. Let me pay it, then; pay it now, before I descend to the valley and all its varieties of desperation." (14-15) The exceptional man of this opening scene of the play turns out to be a "truly weak man" in the next scene. As Bruehl says:

> The Prologue . . . states the central theme of the play—the problem of the exceptional man in relation to society. Is he inevitably corrupted, or can he, by expanding his powers in the contest with impassive nature, escape his dilemma and still find personal fulfilment? Because Ransom is clearly related to Dante's Ulysses the answer of the play is clear: No: By using his exceptional talents in the service of others Ransom is inevitably to be corrupted; and since he foresees

> this inevitability, he is, at the moment he accepts the challenge to climb, like, Ulysses in the eighth circle of Hell, a fraudulent counsellor.[3]

As against the exceptional man in the opening scene of the play, the next scene presents a self-centred, hypocritical, crooked, politically ambitious group led by James Ransom, Michael Ransom's twin brother. This group represents different centres of political power. It is seized with the problem of the threat to the British colonial rule in British Sudoland. There is conflict between Ostnian Sudoland and British Sudoland, two contiguous geographical units. Ostnians have inspired Sudoese to rise in revolt against the British: "Government stores have been burnt, British officers have been attacked. In a few hill stations, the women of the European settlements have been grossly insulted." (19) Lord Stagmantle, who voices the colonial attitude, says: "The truth is that we've got fifty millions invested in the country and we don't intend to budge—not if we have to shoot every nigger from one end of the land to the other. The truth is that we are undergarrisoned and under-policed and that we're in the blue funk lest Ostnians will come over the frontier and drive us into the sea." (21) At this moment James Ransom tells his friends that Ostnians dare not cross over the frontier. The frontier line has the haunted mountain F6 which is guarded by a demon. This fairy tale has turned a legend and the natives have begun to believe that "the white man who first reaches the summit of F6, will be Lord over both the Sudolands, with his descendants, for a thousand years." (22) Ransom concludes that His Majesty's Government is planning to send an expedition to F6 and Michael Ransom has been considered for its leadership.

From the scene described above, we can see that the playwrights have given a specific situation through which they intend to control the responses of the reader. It is a special kind of situation: the fortunes of the Ostnians and the British depend on their control over the native Sudoese. The Ostnian Sudoland and the British Sudoland are separated by "the whole mountain range which culminates in that terrifying fang of rock and ice called so prosaically on our maps 'F6,' but in the native tongue 'Chormopuloda'—that is, the Haunted Mountain. There are many legends about this mountain and the troll who lives on the summit and devours all human beings who dare approach it. No Europeans have, so far, ventured into this region, which is barren to a degree and inhabited only by monks who resent foreigners. These monks practise a mysterious cult which is believed to be descended from the religion of Ancient Egypt" (27) The dialogue leads on towards future action. It is progressive. The playwrights have not only used progressive dialogue, they have used the method of reportage. The radio announcer completes and reinforces whatever was given earlier.

Act I, Scene iii is dramatically very significant. The earlier scene has roused certain expectations in the audience concerning the expedition. The British are planning to send one under the leadership of Michael Ransom. It is a unilateral decision. There is doubt whether Michael will ever accept this responsibility in the light of his pronouncements against Ulysses and Dante in the opening scene of the play. This scene also presents the conflict, both ideological and psychological, between the brothers Michael and James. It also shows Michael's strength in relation to his group which consists in his ability to reconcile opposites, a necessary characteristic of the truly strong man. "Auden has never respected simple-minded revolt as a means of solving a problem. . . . In Auden's eyes, the truest strength lies in the ability to rise above simple opposition to a higher synthesis."[4] Michael Ransom, to be strong, must resist the temptation and negate everything his twin brother James does and is. Early in the play we learn that Michael is an uncompromising idealist, whose fondest dream is to lead the first attempt to climb F6. His temptation arises when his politician brother offers government support for an expedition when F6 suddenly becomes a focal point of international competition for colonial power. Michael refuses for the sake of frustrating his brother and the worldly power James represents: "F6 is my fate . . . but not now. Not like this: No, no, no! I refuse!" (34) Like the Tempters in Eliot's play, James, Isabel and Stagmantle tempt Ransom to accept the leadership of the expedition.

At this moment Michael's mother, who has been summoned by James, comes on the scene and prevails on the climber-son to accept the offer. The encounter between the son and the mother is another important scene in this play. Mrs. Ransom reveals how she has concealed her love for him in order to make him 'truly strong.' To Michael's accusation of a note of preference for James, she says that she fought the temptation to cover baby Michael with kisses: "You were to be unlike your father and your brother/You were to have the power to stand alone;/ And to withhold from loving must be all my love." (38) Denial of filial love has been an obsession with him. Minutes before this encounter, he said to Shawcross: "I shall become as helpless as a baby without its nurse." (31) Finally, Michael yields to his mother, hoping his motives are pure enough to keep the expedition free from taint.

With Act II, Scene ii, the play moves on to an action where the main focus is on Michael Ransom. He is on F6 with his motley group of climbers. His encounter with the Abbot of the monastery, in which his dilemma is discussed at length, "has a force not approached in either of the other plays."[5] Ransom's "dilemma arises from the realization that corruption seems inevitably to follow from the use of power, that the will is usually impure, but that to react therefrom into isolation may be itself another form of sin. By virtue of his qualities, Ransom is potentially a man of power, and he knows this; he is, in fact, obsessed with the problem of power, suspicious of himself, and yet unable to analyze his own motives satisfactorily. He has become profoundly mistrustful of his driving force; he sees the mark of the serpent on all men's actions and on their relations one with another, and his mountain climbing, like his scholar's withdrawal, is in part an escape to a 'purer' battle with impersonal forces."[6]

Ransom and the Abbot dwell deep into the question of man's motives. The Abbot knows that Ransom is aware that life is evil. He points out to him that although he has overcome the temptation of the Demon to blind man to his existence, he should not succumb to another temptation, that is to conquer the Demon and attempt to save mankind. There is the existential dilemma: it is dangerous to become dependent on materialistic views of life, but the temptations of man's will are even more dangerous. These drive man to search for power and power brings evil. This view puts extreme limitations on man's freedom of action, if he does not wish to transgress ethical norms.

Before the discussion of human motives and the corrupted will of man between Ransom and the Abbot, there is the scene in which Ransom and his group look into a crystal ball carried by the Abbot. From the vision of the crystal ball and from his own perspicacity, Ransom knows that the climbing venture will be catastrophic. The Abbot's crystal shows Ransom the special form of his own temptation, in the pleading faces of the lost and lonely who want a healing god and ask Ransom to assume power over them: "Restore us. Restore us to our uniqueness and our human condition." Ransom is haunted by the vision; he has no lack of pity; but he knows that pity can betray, and so produce worse results than it sets out to cure.

The Abbot explains: "The Demon is real. Only his ministry and visitation are unique for every nature." The existence of the demon proves that life is evil and, since the demon works through the will, the will is always impure. One may try to evade the demon or ignore it—like Shawcross, who tried to lose his personality in another's; or one may wrestle with it as Ransom is doing in trying to conquer F6. All these ways, says the Abbot, are wrong: by opposing our will to the demon we bind ourselves more tightly to it. Even the sense of pity is the demon's ally; if Ransom thinks of climbing F6 and then descending to help the world, he will fail:

> As long as the world endures, there must be order, there must be government; but woe to the governors, for, by the very operation of their duty, however excellent, they themselves are destroyed . . . government requires the exercise of the human will; and the human will is from the Demon. (58)

Now Ransom should take a decision about his further course of life. The Abbot offers him an alternative: "To remain here (on the mountain) and make the complete abnegation of the will." (58) When Ransom sees no real solution to his problems, his colleagues decide for him. Thus the tragic error is not only his but it is shared: "The decision to continue his mountaineering expedition, which represents a symbolic attempt to destroy evil, brings about Michael Ransom's defeat, estrangement from his essence, for he is aware that the step is basically wrong."[7] Ransom's decision to go ahead with the ascent is interpreted as a consequence of religious despair:

> Ransom is in a quandary: he wants to climb F6, but recognizes that in doing so he will be playing a corrupt and spurious role. On the other hand, how can he be certain that renunciation of the will is not in itself an act of the will, a subservience to the Demon? Ransom's appeal to "the history and the creator of all these forms in which we are condemned to suffer" reveals at this point what is essentially religious despair.[8]

William J. Bruehl gives a very enlightening reading of the play by examining the "enormous freight of dramatic meaning and a significance" of Polus Naufrangia a unique botanical specimen discovered by Lamp. "Polus Naufrangia, which means Shipwrecked at the Pole, is, of all the symbols in Auden and Isherwood's play, the symbolic key that opens the play's secrets."[9] Lamp is shipwrecked at the pole, since at the moment of triumph, when he finds the unique botanical specimen, he is carried away by an avalanche. There is in the symbol an implicit statement that the broader aspects of man's humanity cannot be sacrificed to extreme scientific specialization. At a different and higher level, Polus Naufrangia functions much more significantly and more profoundly. The playwrights have used this flower as a "symbol of both the action of the play (the attempt to gain knowledge, power and honour through the conquest of the mountain) and the theme (the dilemma of the exceptionally gifted man—how this exceptional man may remain virtuous while committed to the service of society when this service will increasingly augment his power and so ultimately corrupt him)."[10] Polus Naufrangia reveals F6 by relating it directly and unmistakably to the plight of Dante's Ulysses in Canto XXVI of the Inferno. The parallel is this: Ulysses's five-day trip, the Southern Pole, the shipwreck, the mountain of Purgatory, the destructive blast are all deliberately embodied in the five-leaved (five-day trip) flower discovered on a haunted mountain just before the discoverer is swept by an avalanche. Like Ulysses who faces destruction, Michael Ransom dies on F6. Polus Naufrangia is the emblem associating F6 to the Inferno, Ransom to Ulysses.

Scenes ii, iii and iv in Act II are devoted to Michael's relationship with his companions on the mountain. Edward Lamp, devoted to learning, more specifically to botanical knowledge, is meticulous and studious to a fault. He is an example of what scientific specialization implies and what it can cost to the individual. Excessive love of knowledge can be fatal, more so when it is independent of and unrelated to every day concerns of life. Ian Shawcross, overly serious, has a blind devotion to Michael Ransom. Severely critical of frivolity, he is sometimes a victim of jealousy. He doesn't hide his contempt for Gunn and he even wonders at Ransom's patience with him. Ransom's decision not to take him to the summit of F6 so fills him with shame and self-disgust that he jumps over the precipice and dies. As for Gunn, he is overly frivolous, fond of girls, drinks and chocolates. What little humour there is in the play is due to him. Ransom alone has adequate knowledge of Gunn and his capabilities. Ransom says that Gunn is not afraid of death but is afraid of being killed. It is paradoxical that so frivolous and so loquacious a person as Thomas Gunn should become an object of admiration and love of so reticent and so serious, 'scholar and a man of action,' Ransom.

One sees in these characters symbolic suggestions. Auden had attempted such symbolism before, and was to do so again with immense elaboration in *For the Time Being* and *The Age of Anxiety*. Fuller in his perceptive study of the scene remarks that Ransom's four companions symbolize his four faculties: Intuition, Feeling, Sensation and Thought:

> In *F6* Intuition is represented by the Doctor, vegetative and worried about his fatness; Feeling is represented by Shawcross, who is entirely motivated by his hero-worship of Ransom and jealous hatred of Gunn; Sensation is represented

by Gunn, who lives for thrills, sex and fast cars; and Thought is represented by the botanist Lamp, in single-minded pursuit of his Polus Naufrangia. By treating these faculties in isolation in this way, Auden emphasizes the expedition's representation of the imprisoned will. . . . Naturally, this symbolism is hardly one of which an audience would be aware, but it is evidently one of those classifying principles upon which Auden likes to build the development of his themes.[11]

Michael Ransom's followers, disparate and heterogeneous, no doubt symbolize his own four faculties. Just as they differ in temperaments and attitudes, the faculties in Michael are at war with one another. Through most of the play, Michael is shown to be strong enough to hold the opposites together and in balance so that they contribute to the success of the expedition. Inferentially he is able to exercise control over the warning faculties in him. As long as he is in control of himself, the fall is not there yet. The gradual destruction of the group of climbers mirrors the progressive disintegration of Michael. The fall and the tragic end is indicated in the dissolution and death of the group.

The chess game in a fantasy scene presents James as a Dragon and Ransom as a Quest Hero. Ransom is found imagining how his expedition is being exploited by his brother as a panacea for the unhappy lives of the oppressed. They play chess, and though James wins, Ransom, by an appeal to the mysteriously veiled figure on the summit, challenges the victory. James collapses, saying: "It was not Virtue—it was not Knowledge—it was Power." (91) Ransom in his delirium is evidently wishing that his brother might die instead of him, but he blames this guilty fantasy on the veiled figure: "It wasn't my fault! The Demon gave the sign." (92) That is to say, he is not responsible for the conditioning in infancy which made him jealous of his brother.

This is followed by another fantasy scene in which the Abbot sitting in judgment over the case calls the victims of the Demon as witnesses. Shawcross, Gunn, Lamp and the Doctor accuse Ransom of his guilt. Ransom rushes to the Demon's defence. This recognition that the Demon is of his own making, the demon which represents his reasons for climbing the mountain, dismisses the other figures in his fantasy, and leaves him alone at last in peace with the Demon, now unveiled as his mother. He had climbed the mountain to please his mother, and to displace James in her affections. The final moment gives him an illusory triumph.

In the final and the climactic scene located at the summit of F6 where Ransom collapses, the dramatists employ the expressionistic device to reveal the subconscious state of Michael Ransom. The deeper psychological drives of Ransom, his oedipus complex which is at the root of his motivation, his moral corruption, his self-critical analysis are all projected. This is a fine example of dramatic irony in that the outcome is different from what is expected or what may seem fitting. Ransom's feeling of guilt is externalized and in this sense the outcome is different from what is expected. The roles of James and Ransom are reversed now for it is the former who accuses the latter of selfishness.

On the summit, Ransom finds the demon. The demon is real, but is self-created, his own demon; it is finally revealed as Mrs. Ransom, ready to receive Michael on her bosom. She has always given her overt love to James, although her love for Michael was greater. She wanted Michael to learn strength since "the truly strong man is he who stands most alone." But Michael was not sufficiently strong in climbing the mountain, he expressed his desire to displace his brother and possess his mother's love for himself. So he lies destroyed, as the Hidden Chorus sings over him a fine rhetorical dirge on the weakness of man. These implications of the chorus, like that of the discussion with the Abbot, are a good deal wider than any suggested by the Freudian symbolism of the final scene. As Hoggart puts it: "mother-fixation may properly be shown as part of the problem, but to make it the culmination of the whole climb and the climax of the play is to ignore the more complex problems, already posed for the sake of a theatrically startling close."[12]

Barbara Everett commenting on the final scene of the play observes:

> Though the close is certainly the weakest part of the play,

> there is no necessary reason for supposing that this use of the Oedipus complex is a gross mistake; it is a subject that can be made to bear sufficient tragic weight. It can, moreover, equally well be used with satiric force—and the purpose of *The Ascent of F6* is at least as much satiric as tragic; if Auden wanted to exhibit his generation as a collection of infants longing for the consolations of the nursery, he had Brecht's *Rise and Fall of the Town of Mahagonny* to guide him. . . . The difficulty comes, not necessarily through the insufficiency or unlikelihood of the motive cause revealed to illuminate the fatal disease of a man's mind, but in the uncertainty of tone with which the whole situation is handled.[13]

For Blair, the close of the play is an illustration of the schematic structure of the drama. The chess game between James and Ransom, the burlesque court scene held to judge both brothers, the final appearance of Mrs. Ransom at the summit in whose lap Michael lays his head are a "series of set pieces in the form of tableaux," "a passing dumb show" of Michael's subconscious as he nears his death. "In these final scenes the characters lose whatever dramatic reality they have attained and become abstractions. Michael is revealed as a superficially strong man who failed to be "truly strong," a man driven by a hyper-acute Oedipus complex to conceive himself as a heroic world-saviour. James and his cohorts are the world's rulers who gain a hollow power by reconciling the average Mr. and Mrs. A to the lot that offers them."[14]

The fact that there are at least three different endings to the play implies that the playwrights were uncertain about the meaning they wanted the play to embody. The English published text ends differently from the Group Theatre version which in turn differs from the American text. In one the conclusion is political with a broadcast to Mr. and Mrs. A; in the other the conclusion is private, psychological, with Ransom and his mother. These show that they are not only different but are contradictory. If in one the emphasis is on the political success at the expense of the private defeat, in the other the defeat of the tragic hero is played up ignoring political success. As A.R. Humphreys says: "The fact that conclusions with very different implications are apparently thought interchangeable is alarming."[15] But we may justify the dilemma of the playwrights and draw the inference that uncertainty is a condition of the time and of the generation. In Hynes's words, "The problem is essentially a matter of that conflict of public and private themes that was so central to 'thirties writing."[16]

E.M. Forster, who saw the play staged, wrote criticism of the play and sent it to the authors. In his review, he emphasized the plurality of meanings the play embodied. He wrote: "The play is not easy to focus. It is short and straight-forward, yet at least four pairs of spectacles are necessary before we can examine it properly."[17] Forster suggests four ways of reading this play, which amount to four levels of parable: the heroic, the politico-economic, the character test, and the Freudian. He seems right as the play lends itself to multiple readings. In fact, these are the categories of problems that the Auden generation faced and worried about.

At the heroic level, Ransom "is a gifted, sensitive, ascetic, altruistic mountaineer, who covers a noble life with a glorious death. Aeroplanes locate his body on the summit of the virgin peak known as F6, which he alone has scaled. His body perishes, his name liveth for evermore."[18] It is true that Ransom does become a public hero, the "Truly Strong Man" his mother wanted him to become. But like John Nower in *Paid on Both Sides* and the Airman in *The Orators,* he betrays his inner flaw that courage is the public face of private weakness and leadership is a temptation to authoritarianism. An article in the Group Theatre Paper on this aspect of *F6* described Ransom in these words:

> In Ransom, the leader of the expedition to F6, we have a complex study of the hero of action, a figure which has so often attracted the attention of the English theatre. But it is the hero of action in contemporary terms; who reminds us not of Tamburlaine or Agamemnon or Antony, but of T.E. Lawrence, or the dictators of the continent. The pleasant and easy task of lampooning and caricaturing the dictator is here abandoned in favour of an attempt to understand the springs

of his conduct.[19]

At the politico-economic level, the play embodies colonial attitude, its efforts to retain its hold on the natives, its capitalistic interests and its jingoism upholding nationalism. The enthusiasts of the Empire find a scapegoat in Ransom. There is also the theme that power corrupts and the exceptionally gifted man, in this case Ransom, is corrupted by submitting to the will of power-mongers. "The situation is old, the machinery upto date."[20]

There is the third way of reading, the myth of the hero seen from inside, what Forster calls character-test. The play's hero represents an interior journey of self-discovery. This theme and its related theme of heroism turn on the question of whether the hero acts to acquire knowledge of himself, or to gain power and then compensate for his own sense of his inadequacies. Ransom "suffers from the last infirmity of noble minds: thinking he pursues virtue and knowledge, he really pursues power. And at the crisis, in the nightmare-cloud on the summit, he sees that his motive has been impure, and, as evidence of this, the ghosts of the friends whom he has killed. He has sacrificed them in devoting himself. He has tried to turn back, but as soon as he set foot on the mountain all are doomed."[21]

Finally, there is the Freudian level. On the monastery, the Abbot explains to Ransom that the demon takes different forms for its temptations but he does not warn him against the temptation coming in the form of his mother: "When the cloud lifts from the summit of the mountain, Ransom finds his mother waiting for him, reabsorbing that which she has held forth, frustrating that which she has created. He has never escaped her. He re-enters the womb. . . . Mother-love, usually sacrosanct becomes a nasty customer in this exciting play."[22] Auden and Isherwood had treated, in their earlier separate works, mother figures as Freudian carnivores. Both knew a good deal about psychoanalysis.

If the play is read as Freud-oriented, it may be said with Auden that heroes are Truly Weak Men. On the other hand, if read as a propaganda piece, it demonstrates the ugliness of power but it remains ambiguous in stating political alternatives. Leftist critics found the play satisfactorily pro-worker and anti-capit... Lewis, for example, finds the morality of F6 questionab...

> As far as I have understood it, by erecting a colossal bogy out of Lord Action's words "power corrupts . . . all great men are bad," it asserts that the good man's responsibility must begin and end with his own soul. The implications of this are at best Oxford group, and at worst Fascist.[23]

Samuel Hynes, taking into account the contradictory impressions of critics, suggests that *F6* could be taken as "an eccentric tragedy of the between-the-war generation; and like other tragedies, it is not fundamentally concerned with the sort of human problems that can be solved by taking thought or by taking action by joining one group or by denouncing another, but with the problems that are beyond resolution, except by dying. You might call it The Self-Conscious Man's Tragedy, or The Tragedy of the Truly Weak Man, for the essential tragic point is that the self-conscious man strives to discover and judge his own motives, but that, like every tragic hero, he cannot know his motives until he has seen his actions."[24]

Denis Donoghue comparing Yeats's *A Full Moon in March* with *The Ascent of F6* observes:

> They have scarcely anything in common. Yeats's drama appears to exhibit a self-subsistent order, and while we may indicate the relevance of the play to the largest human concerns we recognize also that there was no social event or situation in the 1930's to which the play could be directly referred. Its resonance is not "local." An attempt has recently been made to show that Yeats's last plays spring directly from his conception of the political situation in modern Ireland, but this idea imposes a severe strain on the texts. In *The Ascent of F6*, on the other hand, one finds contemporaneity brandished in theme, diction, and tone. Whereas Yeats looked to an ancient aristocratic theatre-form to enable him to penetrate far below the surface of human life, Auden sought, with the aid of Eliot's *Sweeney Agonistes* a means of remaining on that

surface and cutting through its superficiality. Yeats's impulse was formalist: the force behind Auden was social consciousness.[25]

It is true that social consciousness is the force behind Auden's play but to say that Auden fails to penetrate below the surface of human life is being unfair to the play. The play, as has been pointed out earlier, deals with the perennial questions of man's corrupted will and the motive issuing out of it.

Denis Donoghue, commenting on the structure of *The Ascent of F6*, says:

> *The Ascent of F6* is crudely organized. Dr. Leavis has noted that in this play Auden lacks "the organisation corresponding to his local vitality." Bearing in mind the qualitative parts of a play as Aristotle outlined them, one observes that the diction of *The Ascent of F6* is occasionally impressive, the plot never so; the characters, with the exception of Ransom himself, are ciphers; the play is poor in thought and melody, it offers a certain interest in the "spectacle." The weakness of the plot is particularly serious: instead of inventing a sequence of dramatic situations which would have its own integrity first and thereafter, if he so wished, a moral, Auden merely uses the characters and the plot as allegory. It is symptomatic that in recent discussions of *The Ascent of F6* he has interested himself only in the "meaning" of the play, or the lessons to be drawn from it. He does not reveal any deep concern for the elements of the play as "things," or for their organic coherence, or for the theatre-form which they serve.[26]

The foregoing criticism that the play is crudely organized, that the weakness of the plot is particularly serious, that Auden does not reveal any deep concern for the elements of the play sounds uncharitable. Critic after critic has drawn the attention of the readers to the dramatic and theatrical instincts of Auden as displayed in this play and has judged it the best thirties play. For example, C. Day Lewis thought "the play showed 'marked forward development' from *The Dog Beneath the Skin*, the construction firmer, and the verse no less fine.''[27] *The New Statesman* considered that "the authors had pumped life into a dead literary form and that, in the verse passages, Auden had written some of the best rhetorical poetry of this generation.''[28] *The London Mercury* said: "The play shows a more successful synthesis of literature and propaganda than anything Mr. Auden or Mr. Auden and Isherwood, have yet done.''[29] While the above statements singled out a certain aspect of the play, a note of dissent was struck by Derek Verschoyle in *The Spectator*: "The first act, which ends with Ransom's decision to lead the expedition, is remarkably good; but from that point the play decreases in coherence and force until it dies weakly in the muddle of the final scene.''[30] The observation that the play loses its coherence and force after the first act and dies weakly in the muddle of the final scene needs to be corrected. The concluding part of the play is ironic—the strong man he thought he was proved to be a weakling, the mother-love considered to be sacrosanct is established to be carnivorous, the cries of nationalism and patriotism are fascist in nature. The conflict in the play is dramatized at two levels—physical and mental. At the physical level, the conflict is between Michael Ransom and the group of politicians headed by his brother, James. At the level of subconscious, which is externalized in expressionistic devices, the conflict is between Michael and his mother, his mother and the Abbot of the monasterv. The realistic and the fantastic are cleverly blended.

In conclusion it may be said that it is difficult to accept the charges levelled against the play since it represents an original experiment on the part of Auden to realize a form of dramatic representation that comprises with equal effect and flexibility dialogue and soliloquy, the telescopic and the microscopic, the dithyrambic and the analytical. It is a form admirably suited to the projections of a fusion of private and public themes defining not merely the existence but the existenz.

NOTES

1. 1936 is the peripeteia of the Thirties, the point where the action turned; in that year Hitler reoccupied the Rhineland and the Versailles Treaty was signed; Abyssinia surrendered and League of Nations had failed; the Rome-Berlin Axis was formed and the German-Japanese pact was signed. The Civil war in Spain, a parable of the struggle between the Left and Right, climaxed the tragic fall to disaster and death.
2. *The Ascent of F6 and On the Frontier* (London: Faber, 1937).
3. William J Bruehl, "Polus Naufrangia: A Key Symbol in *The Ascent of F6*," *Modern Drama*, 10 (Sept.), p. 163.
4. John G. Blair, *The Poetic Art of W.H. Auden* (Princeton: Princeton University Press,1965), p. 101.
5. Richard Hoggart, p. 79.
6. *Ibid.*, p. 80.
7. Mirko Jurak, "Commitment and Character Portrayal in the British Politico-Poetic Drama of the 1930s, *Educational Theatre Journal*, 26, 3 (1974), pp. 342-51.
8. John Fuller, A *Reader's Guide to W.H. Auden* (London: Thames and Hudson, 1970), p. 94.
9. Bruehl, p. 161.
10. *Loc. cit.*
11. Fuller, p. 93.
12. Richard Hoggart, p. 82.
13. Barbara Everett, p. 56.
14. John G. Blair, p. 102.
15. A.R. Humphreys, "*The Ascent of F6*," *Cambridgr Review*, 58 (30 April 1937), p. 355.
16. Samuel Hynes, *The Auden Generation* (London: The Bodley Head, 1976), p. 240.
17. E.M. Forster, *Two Cheers for Democracy* (England, Penguin Books, 1965), pp. 268-69.
18. *Ibid.*, p. 269.
19. "The Ascent of F6," *Group Theatre Paper*, 6 (December 1936), p. 5.
20. Forster, p. 263.
21. *Ibid.*, pp. 269-270.
22. *Ibid.*, p. 270.

23. Day Lewis, "Paging Mankind," *Poetry*, 49 (Jan. 1937), p. 227.
24. Hynes, p. 241.
25. Denis Donoghue, *The Third Voice* (Princeton: Princeton University Press, 1959), p. 62.
26. *Ibid.*, p. 68.
27. Charles Osborne, *W.H. Auden: The Life of a Poet* (London: Macmillan, 1982), pp. 138-39.
28. *Ibid.*, p. 139.
29. *Loc. cit.*
30. *Loc. cit.*

On the Frontier: A Melodrama in Three Acts

On the Frontier (1938) is perhaps Auden's unqualified response to the European political crisis—a response which seeks to translate political issues into figures of thought. Considered along with Stephen Spender's *Trial of a Judge* and Rex Warner's *Professor* published in the same year as Auden's play viz., 1938, it might be seen that they exemplify a kind of cultural seismology which is a distinguishing feature of theirs. It is not unusual for works of art to attempt to record the displacements in respect of sensibility that are characteristic of the history of man but very few of them succeeded in registering what seems fundamental to the human spirit. Of the three plays—Spender's, Warner's and Auden's—the last one alone has brought out in personalized terms the elusive quality and character of ideological and national differences and oppositions. The decade preceding the outbreak of the Second World War was charged with a sense of doom which seemed to have found a significant voice in Auden's play—a decade that provided a measure for the very curve of history occasioned by dislocations and discontinuities.

The title of the play *On the Frontier* suggests the great divide as it were between harmony and disharmony, peace and war, confirmation of the value and meaning of life and their denial on which man seems poised refusing to give up his sleep-walking act. It is not merely the political crisis triggered off by failure of Liberalism and Pacifism in the face of Fascism the play is concerned with, but more importantly with the crisis of human compatability brought about by the ideological rather than the ideational considerations. Considered in this perspective the play, *On the Frontier* seems to add a new dimension to the literary artistic representation of unfulfilled, aborted or illustrated love—a dimension that turns a romance into a work of critical realism.

On the Frontier is set against two countries, Westland and Ostnia, one fascist and other monarchist. By extension they could be any two countries between the wars, when Europe witnessed the rise of Nazism and Fascism which dealt a death-blow to the humanity by causing the World War II. Struck dumb at the new phenomenon of rising dictatorships in many parts of the continent, reduced to cynicism in the wake of failure of Liberalism the young intellectuals used artistic medium to represent and satirize the horror, ugliness and boredom of the Thirties generation. Auden and Isherwood's play, satirical and apocalyptic, exposes the follies of leaders and craziness of people.

The play presents two governments opposed to each other and people under the respective governments. The governments are represented by their leaders. Besides the political characters, two representative families are also shown. In fact, the human interest centres round the latter. One interesting innovation of this play is that it presents the two families belonging to the enemial countries simultaneously, not sequentially, on the stage so that "the reactions of the two families can be paralleled and contrasted."[1] The stage is divided into two halves with an imaginary line separating them. As the stage direction says: "It is not to be supposed that the Frontier between the two countries does actually pass through this room: the scene is only intended to convey the idea of the Frontier—the L. half of the stage being in Westland: the R. Half in Ostnia."[2] (130) The stage decoration "ought to show" clearly the distinctness of culture, the attitudes, the economic conditions of the families. Flood lights and focal lights are a part of the dramaturgy suggested to achieve proper effects. When one of the countries is shown, only the respective part of the stage is illuminated. Sometimes both sides of the stage are illuminated to show people on either side and sometimes light is focussed on individual characters. Mrs. Ransom in *The Ascent of F6* is shown in a penumbra of light (II, iii, p. 43) and in the final scenes of that play focal lights concentrate on Michael Ransom.

As in *The Ascent of F6*, the radio and the public address system mediating between the rulers and the ruled become important properties in this play. The abuse of mass media by governments appears to be one of the themes of the plays. Enclosed within the four walls of a house, the people get to know the outside world by means of newspapers and radio. In poverty, people manage with green tea but they insist on their morning newspaper. The Thorvalds watch the progress of the war with the help of newspapers. They are being informed, sometimes misinformed about the facts of war. They know that they are being misled but there is no other way of knowing about the war. The radio blasts and blows information about the war. It works up people to a frenzy. The Leader's voice is heard every now and then. He, being a demagogue, knows the impact of his oratory.

The playwrights use chorus as they had done in *Paid on Both Sides* and *The Dog Beneath the Skin.* In *For the Time Being,* Auden uses Chorus which is ancient and the Narrator who is thoroughly modern. In *On the Frontier,* the chorus whose appearance is rhythmic appears five times—twice in Acts I and III and once in Act II. The chorus comprises factory workers, prisoners, political workers and soldiers. Though they do not participate in the play's action, they provide information otherwise unknown. Compared with other plays, the chorus in this play speaks less number of lines and speaks less impressively:

> The actual choruses are more brief and more detached from main action than in the earlier plays, though they provide a skillfully varied comment from an important social class not otherwise represented in the play, the dissident proletariat. The first chorus . . . is much less expressive, and its very flatness mirrors the weary desperation of industrial regimentation. The next chorus, of prisoners, echoes the repressed defiance of the first in terms which are prophetic without being particularly convincing or inspiring. The rather tired allusion to Shelley's *Mask of Anarchy* in the third chorus, of dancers, similarly suggests that working-class resistance is based on slogans rather than on intelligence or energy. It seems to take the outbreak of war to stir them to action. The

fourth chorus, of soldiers, is much the most sympathetic, and much the most satisfying poetically. The fifth chorus, of newspaper readers, is merely another variation of the rival radios of the scenes in the Ostnia-Westland room.[3]

The play is interspersed with poetry, as in *The Dog Beneath the Skin* and *The Ascent of F6*. Besides the chorus, the verse lines are spoken very appropriately by Eric Thorvald and Anna Vrodny, the pathetic lovers in the plot. While their parents move in opposite directions, the lovers belonging to enemy countries try to come closer. For them the 'frontier' does not exist but unfortunately their attempts to transcend the barrier are marred by their parents. Like their counterparts in love stories of great literature, including Auden's own *Paid on Both Sides*, they meet with the expected end of separation and death. These lovers in their pathetic cries speak in verse. They are poetic characters in the play. Their utterances are charged with emotion and it is but fitting that the dramatists give some fine poetry to them. In contrast, all others who are driven by undesirable moods of jealousy and anger speak prose. Valerian, the armaments manufacturer, the man who dealt in instruments of death, speaks long and speaks most of the prose in the play.

The chorus with which the play opens at the gates of the Valerian Works, the industrial landscape of Westland, speaks before the curtain. The Prologue, unlike the conventional wherein the playwright would beg the audience to take his piece kindly, introduces issues which would unfold themselves in the course of the play. It is spoken by a group of workers, both men and women, appropriately in rhyming couplets. The rhythm of the machine, the rhythm that is imposed on men, are all evoked by the verses spoken by the workers. The prologue is expository in a limited way. It speaks of the predicament of workers, who have been subjected to various kinds of oppression, and of Valerian the industrialist, who has been exploiting the proletariat. There is discontent in the working class which is waiting to strike. However it is very optimistic of its success: "The day is coming, brother, when we shall all be free!" (112) The prologue is communist in content and has 'workers of the world, unite' call for action. In *The Dance of*

Death, Karl Marx appearing at the end of the play pronounces the death of the dancer who symbolizes bourgeoisie: "The instruments of production have been too much for him. He is liquidated." In *On the Frontier,* the pronouncements of the proletariat are explicit in the chorus but the Marxian dialectic of freedom-necessity-choice is implicit in the texture of the play.

Act I, Sçene i has as its setting Mr. Valerian's study. Capitalist that he is, Valerian lives in a charming house filled with treasures. His house symbolically stands on 'high ground' and symbolically overlooks the capital city of Westland. Its furniture and furnishings, the number of statuettes and valuable etchings, the telephones and radiograms speak of Mr. Valerian's riches and his acquisitive tendency. Valerian is a typical capitalist for whom time is money and competence is a by-word. He tells Lessep: "My dear boy, I am never generous—as you will very soon discover to your cost. Please do not flatter yourself that your conscience and its scruples interest me in the very slightest degree. In this establishment, there is no joy over the sinner that repents." (115) In his narcissistic mood of self-gratification and self-absorption, Valerian is gloating over his own remarkable achievements and is totally immersed in his self. As he looks over the Westland industrial landscape, he exclaims: "The Valerian works. . . . How beautiful they look from here! Much nicer than the cathedral next door." In his arrogant self-confidence, he makes fun of the crowd that gathers round factories, working slavishly for their doles, eating in factory cafetaria, sending their children for lesson in "Patriotism and Personal Hygiene," dreaming of "never-never land; where the parks are covered with naked cow-like women, quite free; where the rich are cooked over a slow fire, and the pigeons coo from the enpolas." (116)

Mr. Valerian contemptuously dismisses the workers and their protests as inconsequential:

> Think what you like, vote for whom you like. What difference does it make? Make your little protest. Get a new master if you can. You will soon be made to realize that he is as exacting as the old, and probably less intelligent. . . . The truth is, Nature is not interested ih underlings—in the lazy, the inefficient, the

> self-indulgent, the People. Nor, for that matter, in the Aristocracy, which is now only another name for the Idle Rich. The idle are never powerful. . . . The world has never been governed by the People or by the merely Rich, and it never will be. It is governed by men like myself. (117)

Looking at the photograph of the Leader, he describes him as a "poor muddle-headed bundle of nerves, so overworked and so hypnotized by the sound of your own voice," and dismisses him as one who cannot be the leader. Likewise, he dismisses artists as neurotics and humbugs and says that a creative man becomes an engineer or a scientist, not an artist: "This is probably the last period of human history. The political regimes of the future may have many fancy names, but never again will the common man be allowed to rule his own life or judge for himself. To be an artist or a saint has ceased to be modern. . . . Yes, for the man of power, there can now be but one aim—absolute control of mankind." (118)

In the course of this scene we get to know the political, social and economic conditions in Europe: "England doomed, Germany bankrupt, the United States heading for her last and greatest slump." (119) The conditions are no better in Westland. Stahl, a director in the Valerian Trust, outlines for Valerian how bad things are:

> We're in for really big trouble.
>
> Conditions at the labour camps are getting worse all the time. Men are complaining quite openly: six months ago, they wouldn't have dared. The food isn't fit for an African village. . . . T.B. is definitely on the increase. As for the Shock Troops . . . the whole organization is rotten from top to bottom. The commandants are irresponsibly found in night-clubs and brothels but never report to work. At the barracks . . . the Leader has broken every promise he ever made. The same thing down at the works. Agitators have been getting at the men, secret unions are being formed. (120-21)

Stahl's apprehensions about revolution are confidently dismissed by Mr. Valerian who says that revolution could come in Russia or Spain but never in Westland. He recalls how in Westland when the Emperor abdicated, a cabinet of shop-keepers scrambled to power and took on titles they themselves had just abolished by decree. The worker's expectations were belied when they were described as bolsheviks and traitors. The dictatorship dissolved the parliament and suppressed the unions. Later the Leader came, ruined a number of lesser competitors but did not dare to touch the Valerian Trust. Mr. Valerian is confident that the Leader cannot remain in power even for a fortnight without his support. Equally he is unconcerned and unanxious about the workers's threats: "As for the workers . . . they play at secret meetings . . . and at printing illegal pamphlets. . . . The workers are all patient sheep or silly crowing cockerels, or cowardly rabbits." (122) From the above it may be inferred that the historical moment that Marx had predicted, when capitalist society, its internal pressures perilously strong, is drawing near. None in the play understands what is happening. While Ostnia and Westland blame each other for their troubles and think the other is evil, Valerian dismisses it as nonsense. He seems to think that industrialists and leaders on both sides stage-manage wars to keep the masses docile. Though this is true upto a point, Valerian does not seem to know the entire truth—that forces larger than industrialists and leaders are at work behind wars. As symptoms of capitalism's death rattle, the wars herald a dialectical leap. Valerian knows that proletariat is restive but expects no threat from it.

Valerian-Stahl conversation now centres on the Leader. Valerian has little regard for him and considers him mad. He is cultivating him if only to study the "secret of his success." Asked to clarify the secret, Valerian mockingly says: "The leader, you see, is our national martyr. We Westlanders are a stolid, insensitive race: we need someone to do our suffering for us. The Leader bears upon his shoulders all the wrongs, all the griefs that Westland ever suffered." (124) As they discuss the Leader, the Leader himself arrives to lunch with Valerian. His rhetoric is that of a typical fascist leader. Like a gramophone, he plays his record which is full of platitudes with which Valerian and Stahl are too familiar:

> I am never so happy as when I can spare a few moments from my work to spend among the common people. How delighted and surprised they will be to have their Leader among them! I love to watch their contented smiles as they bend over their humble tasks, working proudly, for Westland, each in his own sphere. How well I understand them! How well I know their wants! I know what they are thinking even before they know it themselves. It is my mission to restore to every Westlander the dignity of labour, to put good honest tools into his hands, to guard him from crafty, underhand foreign competition. Westland must awake! Westland must throw off her fetters! Westland must raise the heavy load of poverty from the shoulders of the groaning poor. (126-27)

Fascism as a symptom of illness has been touched by Auden in *The Dance of Death*. Fascism, according to Auden, seeks to bring to the surface desires long repressed by society but does not attempt cure which lies in destroying capitalist society. Fascism while relieving some of the stress of illness by allowing stored-up resentments noisy but vain expression, acts for the status quo. It strives to sustain capitalism. In *On the Frontier*, "Fascist dictatorship is portrayed as a capitalist ruse for keeping the people in check by the device of "national martyr."[4]

That the Leader indulges in empty rhetoric, that what he says has no relation to what he does, that he is a bundle of contradictions, that what he promises is merely to overcome the fear psychosis in him is all too evident in the song of the prisoners which follows. The handcuffed prisoners, comprising men and women, pour invective on industrialists, on bankers who expect to be saved by the Leader, on the "idle, the rich and the shabby genteel" who believe that "the forces of order have triumphed," on the judge who "talks about all and he talks very big" and on the Leader who stands up on his platform and demanding faith in him and unflinching loyalty to him. The prisoners predict capitalist doom and curse them who talk of "the mystical value of blood," "of war as a holy and purifying flood," and "of bullets and bombs as the true works of art." They are resigned to their fate of dying by a firing squad but are hopeful that History has other ideas and Time is patient: "For Truth Shall flower and Error explode/And the people be free then to choose their own road." (129)

The opening scene of the play lays bare the political atmosphere of the Westland. The fascist dictatorship under the control of capitalism has created discontent not only among military ranks and but also among people at large. The Leader appears bold, puts on an air of confidence, although he fears his position. He is a kind of neurotic, a bundle of nerves, who always tries to shake off his shakiness by his oratory. Even the industrialists whom he protects against the workers hate him. Valerian, the industrial magnet, Stahl, another industrialist, consider him an idiot and forebode his fall. The chorus of workers and the chorus of prisoner, which appear before and after the opening scene, reinforce the meaning derived by the spectators about the Westland condition. The capitalist society is guilty of crimes against not only workers but common men as well. The highly charged choral verses speak of the economic and moral decay of the fascist society.

If Act I, Scene i introduces the Leader, Scene ii introduces the led. The playwrights show the consequences of the Westland fascist dictatorship on the men in the country. A microcosmic unit, a family, is presented. As a parallel and a counterpart to this Westland family, an Ostnian family is also presented. The presentation is not sequential but simultaneous. At one and the same time, we see both families on the stage, each occupying one half of the stage. The characters on each side are not conscious of their counterparts. Only Eric of the Westland and Anna Vrodny of Ostnia seem to be aware of each other's presence. Simultaneous presentation of two families of rival countries on the stage is a novel device employed by the playwrights.

The play attempts contrasting and mutually exclusive political and cultural seismology. It also presents a resolution—a resolution which is ironical. That no system is good and all suffer from serious limitations. If they succeed at all, they do so only negatively: people are indoctrinated to hate people of another country and are persuaded to love the systems of their respective governments. It is in their selfish interests that heads of governments always seek war and sustain it so that people have but one thought—the thought of war. While the leader busies himself saving the nation from war, he successfully evades the real issues. The people suffer from want, unemployment, sicknesses, disease and death.

Mutual recriminations is the theme of Act I, Scene ii. Dr. Thorvald, the University Professor, belonging to Westland, is seriously upset over the degeneration in academic sphere. He is annoyed at the plagiarism and false scholarship of an Ostnian scholar, Professor Jongden. He remarks: "All superficial brilliance and fluff, with nothing behind it. No Ostnian ever made a scholar." (131) His prejudice against the Ostnians colours his judgment of things Ostnian. He tells his son Eric, who has been preparing an essay on "The Chances of European Peace," that it is a ridiculous subject: "You are wasting your time, my boy, what chances are there of peace—with the Ostnians arming to the teeth? I tell you, Europe's Powder-magazine. It only needs a spark." (132) Dr. Thorvald also says that war is imminent but Eric Thorvald, hopeful and optimistic, doesn't think so: "Of course there'll be a war if we all go on saying and thinking there will be, and doing nothing to stop it." (133) Even though the Thorvalds say that Ostnians "are jealous of our liberty and power of creative progress," "A decadent race is always jealous of a progressive one," Eric suggests that "if people—the ordinary decent people in both countries—would only get together," they can prevent war. He dismisses the cynical pastor, who chose for his sermon "I come not to bring peace, but a sword," as unchristian. Eric is one who believes "They that live by the sword shall perish by the sword." (135) Looking at the Leader's picture intently he grasps the meaning. Behind the fierceness of the Leader's eyes there is, Eric says, yearning for love. The Vrodnys of Ostnian on their part accuse the Westlanders of inciting war. They think that the Ostnian ought to have vanquished them in the recent war. All the Ostnian ills are attributed to the Westlanders. The strikes in the docks, the local agitations are all inspired by them.

Act II, Scene i depicts war-nerves and war of nerves. People on either side watch the war which has been declared. There is fear, anxiety and excitement over the fighting. Children are killed by bombings. Old men are killed by war planes. People are crying for revenge. The Westland and Ostnian radios are flashing news bulletins about the progress of war and about the steps taken by the respective governments. Thorvalds and Vrodnys are swearing against their enemies. There are demonstrations, destruction of enemies's properties, in both countries. The only persons who refuse to get excited and remain sober and pensive are Eric Thorvald and his sweet-heart, Anna. Each complains of headache and remains silent. The Westland students march along the streets praising the Leader and the Ostnian Air Cadets swear that they will save their country before they die. Meanwhile, the Westland and the Ostnian broadcasting stations broadcast the Leader's and His Majesty's speeches, which are listened to in rapt attention. Col Hussek an Ostnian is so worked up that he breaks down but is revived, ironically, by Westland whisky.

When people on either side of the stage disappear tired and out, Eric and Anna draw close to each other. Their meeting is one of the finest moments in the play. In a play where there are so many disgusting things like war, one is relieved to hear such fine poetry. One is reminded of the world famous lovers whose innocence is a victim of ruthless society. The lovers speak as the sad and unhappy inheritors of a wasteland which is the scene of calumny, hatred, jealousy, fear. Man has made a mess of things. He dreams of a Utopia but converts it into a rats's alley. There is no place for love and lovers. The only place which is ideal is the place which escapes man's search light:

> This is the good place
> Where the air is not filled with screams of hatred
> Nor words of great and good men twisted
> To flatter conceit and justify murder.
> Here are no quarrels or public meetings,
> No disease or old age. No death.
> Here we can be really alone,
> Alone with love, and faith, and knowledge. (150)

In Act II, Scene ii, Valerian and Stahl are shown listening to the vow of the Leader, who is speaking to the nation over the radio.

Reacting to it, Valerian says that no one wants war—the industrialists, the politicians and not even the general staff. It is difficult to locate the cause or identity the person causing war. While Valerian and Stahl discuss the Leader's plan at mobilization, the Leader surprises them appearing himself in person. What follows is an instance of self-pity. The Leader admits to being a victim of circumstances. Leadership "is a terrible burden to put upon the shoulders of one man . . . you think I am strong? No, I am weak, weak. . . . I never wished to be the Leader. It was forced upon me . . . by the men who said they were my friends, and who thought only of their ambition. They made use of me. They made use of my love for my dear country." (159) The Leader narrates the stunning story of a peasant boy, a bank clerk out of job, whose parents gave their last savings to have him educated, a boy who was afraid of the world, of the rich people in their fine houses and who by his oratory step by step climbed higher and higher, became cunning, did horrible things like intrigue and murder. Now the Leader feels guilty and trembles. The story is his own. He wants to be alone, be humble and free. He breaks into tears. As he listens to the record of Rameau's Tambourin, a change comes over him. He announces his decision to suspend war and withdraw Westland troops unconditionally, ten miles from the frontier: "War is glorious, but Peace is more glorious still." (161) Even as he prepares himself for the Peace Speech and even as he prepares to offer the gift of peace to the world, he is informed of Ostnian aggression on Westland, of foul and heartless murder of women and children. The Leader suddenly becomes hysterical and cries: "The die is cast! The name of Ostnia shall be blotted from the map of Europe for ever!" (161)

If in Act II, Scene i the playwrights define the good place, the everlasting garden, where innocence and love "walk together always/Happy, happy, happy, happy," in Scene ii they define the truly weak man as against the truly strong man. All fascist leaders, dictators are weak. They have "cold funk (which) is an exceedingly dangerous state of mind." They put on masks of boldness and resort to heroics to cover up their "dangerous state of mind." Though they are surrounded always by men of rank and honour, they feel lonely and desolate. They are overburdened by people's love and faith that peace or war is entirely their own choice.

In Act III, Scene i, the curtain rises above the Ostnia-Westland Room. There is a gap of nine months between the earlier scene and this one during which the rival nations have been fighting a war. Instead of preparations for war as in the earlier scenes of Act II, there are now consequences of war. The Thorvalds are badly ruined. The women are rolling bandages, knitting mufflers while Dr. Thorvald is reading casualty-lists. The Vrodnys, on the other hand, sit mourning the dead—Colonel Hussek and Oswald. The effects of war are more terrible and disastrous on Mrs. Vrodny. As the scene opens, she is seen "all in black, alone. She is staring in front of her, with a fixed expression. She looks much older." (165) Besides mental agony caused by deaths, there is poverty, an inevitable consequence of the war: "War seems so beastly when it actually happens! Perhaps 'country' and 'frontier' are old-fashioned words that don't mean anything now." (166-67) Dr. Thorvald wonders as to why countries fight against each other. He tells his wife that he has been "brought up to think that a man's greatest privilege was to fight for his country; and it is hard to change one's ideas." (166) The notions of nationalism, heroism, patriotism have been bred into his system. He, along with his sister Martha Thorvald, finds fault with his son Eric for his pacifist ideals. Even he, who puts the country above self and family, runs away from his sister when she is affected by plague. But we are to understand that he cannot escape death. We hear no more of Thorvalds.

Mrs. Vrodny and Anna, reduced to rags, compelled to mortgage what they have, are unable to keep balance. Anna cries hysterically: "Can't they do anything to stop it, before it kills everybody in the world? It's taken grandfather. It's taken Uncle Oswald. It'll take us, too, soon! What have we all done that we should be destroyed like this? Nobody's alive any more! I look at the faces in the streets, and they're not the faces of living people! We're all dead!" (168) Mrs. Vrodny tries to pacify her daughter but, like Nora in *The Riders to the Sea,* passionately grieves over successive deaths in her family: "Grandfather was a soldier, and his father before him. We're the only ones left now. Perhaps we shan't be here much longer." (169) Thorvalds and Vrodnys may be called sacrificial victims for they are killed for no fault of theirs. They live during peace and die when there is war. They can choose neither peace nor war and they merely accept what is chosen for them by the leadership.

In Act III, Scene ii, Valerian is shown nervously pacing up and down in his study. His servant, Lessep, is killed by plague. Besides the Westland-Ostnia war, there is a civil war in both the countries. The workers in Tambeg Colliery, one of his concerns, have struck work and have threatened to destroy the plant. He is cut off from the front as the "storm must have broken down the wires." Stahl brings the news that the "whole Northern sector has mutinied and are fraternizing with the enemy. All officers who tried to stop them were shot out of hand." (177) The eruption of civil war comes as a surprise to the complacent Valerian but it has been forecast by the soldiers from both sides who sang in unison: "We are sick of the rain and the lice and the smell,/ We're sick of the noise of shot and shell,/And the whole bloody war can go to hell!" (174)

Stahl also gives an account of happenings in Ostnia: "There was a revolution in the Ostnian capital this morning. The King's hiding somewhere in the mountains; tomorrow he will have abdicated, if he is alive. The Ostnians have got loudspeakers in the front line, calling on their soldiers to make an armistice and revolt against their own government!" (177) Stahl persuades Valerian to flee from Westland who refuses instantly. He blames the General, Hammel, for dragging on the war for nine months. The plague is bad luck. As for mutinies and strikes, they are bound to be there: "There were plenty in the Great War." Valerian expresses the hope that once the Leader visits the trenches, the soldiers make an advance somewhere, "the papers will predict an immediate victory, and the workers and the soldiers will go back to their jobs." (178) Stahl tries to convince Valerian that the civil war cannot end. But Valerian is so confident of the failure of "a rabble of half-baked townees and farm labourers." As he scornfully dismisses the attempts of working classes to subvert capitalists as futile and worthless, he is overtaken by Storm-Trooper Grimm, who has been waiting for an opportunity to avenge his dismissal from Valerian works and also the deaths of his parents, whose bankruptcy was the result of

Valerian big business. Valerian is told that the Leader is lying "with his face on the table and twenty bullets on his back." Valerian now tempts Grimm with money but to no avail. He refuses to seek forgiveness and offers to be killed by Grimm. His awareness of the revolutionary proletariat and his understanding of Marxian dialectic have not made him anticipate his own fall—capitalism's death rattle.

The dream scene, an expressionist device used by Auden already in *Paid on Both Sides* and *The Ascent of F6*, at the end of the play presents the pathetic lovers Anna and Eric, he succumbing to a wound caused by "the swift impartial bullet" and she to the plague she caught while nursing the sick. It conjures before us the great tragic scenes in world literature where the star-crossed lovers meet with a fatal end for no fault of theirs. Anna cries agonizingly:

> Will people never stop killing each other?
> There is no place in the world
> For those who love. (189)

Eric dies hopefully:

> But in the lucky guarded future
> Others like us shall meet, the frontier gone,
> And find the real world happy. (190)

He is dreaming of a Utopia and looking forward to the millennium:

> To build the city where
> The will of love is done
> And brought to its full flower
> The dignity of man. (191)

This scene roused mixed reaction in the critics. For Hynes, the last lines of the play are particularly striking in that they deflect our attention from politics to a theme beyond politics. He remarks:

> The final sixteen lines, spoken antiphonally by Eric and Anna

(or to be precise by their spirits, since they are both dying in separate hospitals at the moment), are particularly striking in the way they anticipate Auden's later writing—poems, for example, like "In Memory of W.B. Yeats" and "Sept. 1, 1939."[5]

For McEachran these lines look "uncommonly like a Christian hymn to a better world."[6] They are Auden's farewell to the thirties.

Louis MacNeice, commenting on the sentimental love scenes at the end of the play, says that the "mystical love scenes of Eric and Anna made one long for a sack to put one's head in."[7] In fairness to the play, it may be pointed out that it is a convention of melodrama that the language and emotion are over-emphasized and overdone. Moody Prior justifies the introduction of verse in the final scene of the play. She says:

> Useful verse is here not only to give to the sentiments of the young people greater poignancy, but also to distinguish their hope and idealism from the hard, benighted confusion which runs throughout this play. . . . The device is effective in a theatrical way; it is striking, ingenious, and makes an immediate attack on the emotions. But it illustrates the difficulty of the merely occasional use of verse. The critical intelligence of Auden and Isherwood has already been too much for it; in the context of the almost unrelieved anatomizing and irony which precedes, this sudden affirmation of faith and hope seems like the pathetic and misguided immaturity of the adolescent youngsters, Anna and Eric, rather than the concluding sentiment of the play.[8]

In the unpublished text of the play, written in 1937, there seems to be a choral report of the workers's victory in the civil war. After their return from China in 1938, Auden and Isherwood revised their political forecast. They seemed to have lost hope in workers's triumph and they also apprehended that Soviet and Fascist intervention would threaten a world conflict. "Although the finished play makes a perfunctory tribute to the workers' struggle in the choruses for activists and prisoners, the verse is far too tired to take seriously. As with *F6*, there are no demands for action and no Brechtian challenges to alter history. The forces described are too large and uncontrollable for the audience to find any hope of changing them.''[9] In the context of the revision and the altered ending which reads like a Christian hymn to a better world, it may be said that Auden was slowly moving away from politics.

On the Frontier has been called ''a melodrama in three acts'' much to the annoyance of the drama critics, since it is hard to apply the label Auden has given to the play. For in a melodrama traditionally incidents of improbability abound. As a matter of fact, melodrama is the carrying through of dramatic principles to their logical extremes. It ''goes to extremes as a sort of short cut to its goal, which is to reward the virtuous and punish the wicked; it eschews subtlety in favour of improbability, the more sensational the better.''[10] *On the Frontier* cannot be described strictly as a melodrama. The play is realistic in that it reflects the political and social conditions of the thirties. Heroes as well as villains die and there is neither peripeteia nor deus ex machina to rescue the good from the bad. One might label this play a tragedy since no one survives at the end—the war and the plague wipe out all.

Barbara Everett considers *Frontier* free from some of the ''eccentricities'' of *F6* and says that the playwrights ''present something far more accomplished, though in a more conventional dramatic technique, in which many of their most characteristic talents are largely subdued.''[11] It is true that it reads like a conventional play with specific situations which have extensive significance. The main action centres in two characters—Valerian and the Leader. It is they who determine the fates of men and women. The Leader in the *Frontier* is half mad—one moment he wants to suspend war, the next moment he craves for it. There is the conflict within him. With a limited number of characters and a concentrated piece of action confined to a limited number of places, the play achieves concentration and tightness. There is a naturalness in the dialogues since the playwrights employ different levels of speech and different kinds of rhythm. The verse couplets of the workers, the lyrical effusions of Eric and Anna, the rhetoric of the Leader and

Valerian, all speak of the fact of the playwrights who seem guided by suitableness to the person, to the occasion and to the effect to be secured.

For Hoggart, *Frontier* is "a very tidy piece" but has, in contrast with *The Dog*, "much less sparkle." "We are presented with an animated cartoon on the quarrels of national states, the machinations of international capitalists,the deceptions of the Press, the psychology of fascism and the inner decay of the democracies."[12] He objects to the long soliloquy of Valerian on the common man, cared-for and unfree and observes that the playwrights ought to have omitted such things or to have realized them in terms of incident. Auden, it may be remembered, does not try to create dramatic illusion. If anything, he tries to break the illusion and to make the spectators think. Valerian's long speech is a historical survey of the birth of Capitalism and the inner contradictions in it. A play in which proletarian problems are central, such a view as Valerian's serves as a background.

Samuel Hynes comparing *Frontier* with *Trial of a Judge* observes that "in its political content the play (*Frontier*) is less simplified, and less propagandist than Spender's is." "The subject of *On the Frontier*," Hynes continues, "is the way war starts, and the follies and suffering of ordinary people in war. The combatants are two invented European states, one fascist and one monarchist, and because the authors found neither system desirable they could withhold political partisanship, and attach their sympathies to the victims on both sides. The play is in fact against both states, because it is against nationalism as a cause of war."[13] The perspective that Hynes provides is interesting in that the play does not emphatically show that the proletariat have risen in revolt to destroy the capitalists. On the other hand, there is the imperative suggestion that fascist dictatorship is responsible for the war. For this reason the play "is not," as Hynes argues, "focussed on individual charaters, but is rather a contrapuntal structure of groups: the industrialists and their Leader, two ordinary families on opposite sides of the frontier, the People (workers, prisoners, soldiers, newspaper readers), and lovers—all helpless, all moved by events beyond their control. The momentum of the play is in the movement of the two countries into war, but no human character wills that movement."[14] Hynes finds support for his reading in MacNeice who in his review of *Frontier* says that there are "series of melodramatic cartoons . . . like a number of escaped posters and photographs blown by the wind in one's face."[15] He says that MacNeice's image is an apt one, for "the public action grows more and more chaotic as war approaches—as though war were simply another name for the end of all order. The final 'cartoon' is a scene in which five men read contrapuntally from five newspapers of different political positions, each with its own view of the chaos of Europe. They are mutually contradictory as to causes, but agreed as to consequences—a World War. It is the apocalypse, as reported in the press."[16]

Fuller says that *Frontier* in its political awareness is "less suggestive" than its predecessors: "It is urgent, dramaturgically neat and quite sincere: but it lacks a myth. It is a play which leaves no clear images in the mind. . . . The final impression of the play is that the millions who suffer are not in control of their destiny, and that despite the broadly Marxist terms of the political analysis, the 'full flower and dignity of man' will not be attained without the 'will of love.' As agents of that will, Eric and Anna dwell uneasily within the brisk realism of their dramatic context, and the tone of their final Liebstod points forward—in its stylistic gestures towards emotions, as distinct from a stylistic embodiment of emotion—to the medium of opera."[17]

On the Frontier exemplifies a kind of melodramaturgy that has not been attempted by any other English writer and which offers a comment on modern composers of operas since it steers clear of what may be termed a primitive proto music in its bid to restore to drama its original dithyrambic quality or character.

NOTES

1. Monroe K. Spears, p. 103.
2. *Ascent of F6* and *On the Frontier* (London: Faber, 1938), p. 130.
3. John Fuller, pp. 97-99.

4. Herbert Greenberg, *Quest for the Necessary: W.H. Auden and the Dilemma of the Divided Consciousness* (Cambridge: Harvard University Press, 1968), p. 84.
5. Samuel Hynes, pp. 310-11.
6. F. McEachran, "Topical Drama" *Adelphi*, 15 (January 1939), p. 202.
7. Louis MacNeice, quoted in Hynes, p. 309.
8. Moody E. Prior, *The Language of Tragedy* (Bloomington: Indiana University Press, 1950), pp. 371-72.
9. Edward Mendelson, p. 294.

For the Time Being: A Christmas Oratorio

Published in 1944 at the height of the Second World War, Auden's *For the Time Being*[1] strikes a note that is distinct from what any of his earlier works does—a note of Christian pietism which is not surprising in view of the circumstances concerning its composition. Its sub-title "Christmas Oratorio" draws attention to the occasion for which it was specifically intended and also to the character of the composition although an abridged version was set to music by the American composer Melvin Levy. Moreover, it was dedicated to his mother Constance Rosalie Auden who was an extremely devout and pious Christian whose piety had a lasting effect upon Auden's sensibility which was otherwise irreverent and skeptic—intellectualist. Considered from this standpoint *For the Time Being* presents an interesting perspective on T.S. Eliot's *Murder in the Cathedral* which is indisputably one of the great plays of the present century. While the theme and the very form of *Murder in the Cathedral* seem to have been evolved out of the Christian religion and ritual, *For the Time Being* is content with the exploitation of their form and spirit. However, Auden's play does signal as Eliot's does the return to one of the earliest and original sources of drama and the restoration of poetry to the English stage. The juxtaposition of these two plays seems justified in that they spell the character of a kind of English drama which has achieved a remarkable fusion of ancient and modern of great significance—dramatic and dramaturgical. The differences between them relate to the different ends to which they are directed although they both offer a telling comment on human reality. Auden's seems to have steered clear of the specific implications which a Christian composition necessarily has in order to realize a texture that would find favour with even the most radical of both believers and non-believers. It is, therefore, not surprising that the issues framed by the play though essentially religious and moral are discussed in terms which had been familiarized by empirical theologians and existentialist thinkers concerned with both spiritual and socio-cultural aspects of human condition.

Divided into nine parts, *For the Time Being* seems patterned on the Nativity story as projected in medieval drama. However, the significance of this division in Auden's play owes little to what is hallowed in Christian celebrations of medieval drama since it attempts to telescope the whole of human history in terms of the different displacements which occurred not only at the time of advent of Christ but also at other times including the present as a result of man's inability to cope with the challenges of both life and history. As the title indicates, the interregnum between the birth of Christ and the Good Friday, that is between Promise and Fulfillment, seems endless in that man has remained alienated both from himself and God as he had been in the pre-Christian era which state is marked by a kind of hopeless despair and frustration and even metaphysical anxiety. The different sections or divisions denote more the stations of the Cross as Jesus moved towards his Crucifixion than those of enlightenment and hope which the Nativity legend connotes. Modern man's cross is of his own choosing and making and hence he feels responsible for it and suffers it while seeking redemption from it. The play as such does not focus on the redemptive choices open to man but on the complex fate which is highlighted by the play of light and darkness characterizing his engagement with life. From a post-Nietzschean point of view, this work would appear to be an attempt to resolve Nietzsche's paradox ("God is dead") in a Christian way. In other words, there is the implied suggestion that the history of Being begins almost inevitably with the forgetting of Being which is what accounts for modern man's predicament and also for his existential despair. The distinction of this work lies not in the presentation of a kind of poetic history of theodicy but in the framing of it in terms of the Mephistophelean question whether the world is indeed attuned to man's happiness or redemption.

For the Time Being[2] opens on a contemporary setting. As a work primarily expressing faith in the Incarnation of the Son of God, it seeks to present an analogy between the present and past religious experiences as well as between particular and universal problems. The use of colloquial diction in the oratorio points to the relevance of the Nativity legend to the contemporary situation. The chorus and the narrator speak alternately in formalized style and conversational manner respectively. They are also differentiated from each other by their metres, rhythms and imagery. While the chorus describes the past, the narrator goes beyond the poem to comment on the contemporary situation.

The oratorio form of *For the Time Being* is found to be appropriate for Auden's purpose—that of awakening the consciousness of the spectators to their real condition. They are constantly made aware of the singing voices on the stage and the characters those voices represent. By this Auden seems to be seeking an effect he sought in the plays. The absence of dramatic illusion, identification and characterization contributes to a built-in alienation effect. From the religious point of view, the form of the Christmas oratorio embodies "three kinds of meaning: (1) the Unique Incarnation; (2) by association with Christmas and with other Christmas oratorios, plays, pageants, and the like, the annual attempt in Christendom to apprehend and experience the event as the centre of the Christian year; (3) the constant attempt of Christians to understand, make viable,and in some sense repeat the Incarnation in their daily lives."[3] Since the oratorio succeeds in enclosing all the above suggestions, it may be said that the choice of the form is imaginative and purposeful.

"Advent," the opening section of the oratorio, describes the world before Christ's birth. The chorus sings:

> Darkness and snow descend;
> The clock on the mantelpiece
> Has nothing to recommend,
> Nor does the face in the glass
> Appear nobler than our own.
> As darkness and snow descend

On all personality. (133)

The images of darkness and snow effectively suggest old world's spiritual vacuum and despair. The semi-chorus expresses disillusionment with the secular rule:

Can great Hercules keep his
Extraordinary promise
To reinvigorate the Empire?
Utterly lost, he cannot
Even locate his task. (133)

There is the implied answer that Hercules, the secular saviour, can save neither himself nor the world from despair. The men are haunted by the fear of death:

The evil and armed draw near;
The weather smells of their hate,
And the houses smell of our fear;
Death has opened his white eye
And the black hole calls the thief
As the evil and armed draw near. (135)

The narrator also admits to the awfulness of the situation but knows that people do not know how to overcome the horror:

We are afraid
Of pain but more afraid of silence; for no nightmare
Of hostile objects could be as terrible as this Void.
This is the Abomination. This is the wrath of God. (137)

In reply to the narrator's ironical account of man's despair, the chorus comments: "Alone, alone, about a dreadful wood/Of conscious evil runs a lost mankind." Man wants to know "Where is that Law for which we broke our own,/Where now that Justice?" Why has "The Pilgrim way . . . led to the Abyss?" Man dreads the "Goodness" of God and is now afraid that it might not be good. The

Law instead of revelation brought him to the abyss and failed him to glimpse "that Wholly Other Life." The Recitative which follows does not attempt a solution. It merely catalogues the seemingly impossible conditions for the occurrence of the miracle. It suggests that man must learn to live without feeling, without hope, without accidental virtue and above all without self-consciousness. Man is asked to "see without looking, hear without listening, breathe without asking," and to believe that "The Real is what will strike you as really absurd." (138)

It has been pointed out that the narrator's speech and the Recitative have something of Eliot's influence. Parallels between the horror experienced by Charles in *The Family Reunion* in the waiting room of the country junction and the horror felt by the narrator in the "Advent" testify to this.[4] Nelson remarks that "there is the dramatic conflict in the Advent section in that when man asks for reasons or help, he seems to get only riddles in reply. From this point the work moves in two directions: 1) inside man as an individual; 2) into the activity of the world outside. Auden uses this double movement in order to present the fact of the Incarnation and individual reactions to it."[5]

The second section "The Annunciation" employs the medieval morality tradition of personifying abstractions. The idea of dissociation of sensibility, so central in the seventeenth-century poetry as pointed out by Eliot, is used here. The four faculties—intuition, feeling, sensation, thought—were once one but were dissociated by the Fall. The four signify a split of flesh and spirit, consciousness and unconsciousness in man. Together they are the "Ambiguous causes/Of all temptation" and "lure man either/To death or salvation." As they look into the garden, each describes its vision in cynical tones. It is appropriate that this part is introduced by the four faculties because their separate existences symbolize man's lack of wholeness. If man is to recapture the unself-conscious natural innocence, he must attain that wholeness of personality which was fragmented by the Fall.

The Annunciation proper, expressed in a series of beautiful lyrics, makes the parallel with Eve in the Garden of Eden:

When Eve, in love with her own will,
Defied the will of Love and fell,
She turned the flesh Love knew so well
To knowledge of her love until
Both love and knowledge were of sin:
What her negation wounded, may
Your affirmation heal today. (146)

Gabriel tells Mary that she has been chosen to do "the will of Love," to repair Eve's sin and that to her is given the opportunity of being an instrument for the redemption of man. Mary is given the opportunity to bring Love itself and love of self together so that "Love's will on earth may be, through you,/No longer a pretend but true." She must affirm what Eve negated by accepting Love's will. Mary rejoices that God,

As a pledge of His word to love her
Against her will, and to turn
Her desperate longing to love,
Should ask to wear me,
From now to their wedding day,
For an engagement ring. (146)

This is a very significant part of the poem since it touches on important aspect of man's relationship to God. Man's innocence lies in accepting life, not in seeking knowledge.

In contrast to the exalted, majestic and intense lyrics of Gabriel and Mary, the diction in the next section "The Temptation of St. Joseph" is thoroughly modern. Here are images which suggest parallelism between Joseph's doubts and the absence of faith in the modern world. Joseph is presented as a familiar medieval dramatic character. Auden uses Joseph as an example of someone who needs an "important and elegant proof" for believing, someone who is hesitating to take the leap of faith. Joseph is troubled by doubts about Mary's honour:

All I ask is one
Important and elegant proof
That what my Love had done
Was really at your will
And that your will is Love. (151)

The narrator is critical of Joseph's attitude, "the attitude which becomes defiant or resentful or querulous in face of the demand to believe without safe assurances, which would like to keep the Truth down to its own cynical level, and which reduces any manifestation of Love to a bar room joke."[6] His comments on the relations between sexes are amusing. He concludes saying Joseph and Mary must be man and wife as if nothing had happened since faith abolishes the distinction between the usual and the exceptional: "To choose what is difficult all one's days/As if it were easy, that is faith. Joseph, praise." (153)

This section ends with a brilliant semi-chorus invoking Joseph and Mary to pray for various types of sinners. First there are "those/ Misled my moonlight and the rose,/For all in our perplexity." This is an obvious reference to the romantic lovers who hope to regain innocence through knowledge of the flesh, and believe "Simultaneous passions make/One eternal chastity." There are "independent embryos" (children in the womb) whose original sin is seen even in the "germ-cell primary division." And then, the bourgeoisie, the "proper and conventional," whose "loves/Acquire so readily/The indolent fidelity/Of unaired beds," whose "Domestic hatred can become/A habit forming drug" and whose "self-respect is tempted/To incest not adultery." Finally, Joseph and Mary are invoked to "Redeem for the dull the /Average way." The "Common ungifted natures" faced with temptations like the above now cry for help to face the Summons.

Commenting on the ingenious juxtaposition of the ancient and the modern in "the Temptation of St. Joseph," Nelson remarks:

> What Auden has effected here is perhaps the neatest welding together of past and present in the whole of *For the Time Being*. Joseph is seen as modern, anxious man. Afraid of

> being a cuckold because of both personal pride and fear of public ridicule, he is not given answers to assuage his fears. Instead, he is told, as though instructed by Kierkegaard, that he must feel anxious because man is sinful; and, moreover, he must praise God not in spirit of but because of his anxiety. . . . Joseph is thus the first Christian, the first man who is told not to question but to accept the Incarnation, because there is no way for him to understand.[7]

It has been shown in the earlier pages how much Auden owes to Kierkegaardian Christianity. Kierkegaard seems to have provided the theological and aesthetic scaffold to Auden's longer poems.

The next section "The Summons" contrasts human wisdom with Christian revelation. The inadequacy of speculative philosophy represented by Magi and the inadequacy of ancient political statecraft represented by Caesar are described here. The parallel between the year of Christ's birth and modern times is explicit and the diction more modern than ancient. As Spears observes here Auden "has the special problem of avoiding both the powerful influence of Eliot's 'Journey of the Magi' and the cliches of Christmas pageants."[8] However, he transfers the traditional solemnity of Magi to the star which pronounces the doom of classical wisdom of moderation. "The Summons" is to the high and the low, to Caesar, to the Wisemen and the Shepherds. It is a summons to face the Truth. The Star announces to the Three Wise Men who are following it, each for his own reason—the first because he failed to see the Truth by the scientific examination of nature; the second because he put his faith in the constant flow of Time, but discovered the present no better; the third because he set store by abstract intellect and found himself incomplete. The first follows the star "to discover how to be truthful now"; the second "to discover how to be living now"; and the third "to discover how to be loving now." These three men "know for certain that we are three old sinners" and so after the journey seek "To discover how to be human now." To them the Star gives the advice:

> Descend into the fosse of Tribulation,

Take the cold hand of Terror for a guide;
Below you in its swiling desolation
Hear tortured Horror roaring for a bride:
O do not falter at the last request
But, as the huge deformed head rears to kill,
Answer its craving with a clear I Will;
Then wake, a child in the rose-garden, pressed
Happy and sobbing to your lover's breast. (159)

The narrator now introduces the voice of the secular state. Caesar's proclamation which is followed by a Fugal-chorus in ironic praise of him. The state is more our own than that of Augustus, the seven kingdoms Caesar has conquered are the man's achievements: Abstract Idea which includes everything from language to philosophy; Natural cause is natural sciences; Infinite Number is mathematics; Credit Exchange is monetary system; Inorganic Giants are machines; Organic Dwarfs are drugs; the Popular Soul is mass media. The narrator ironically implies that the material world is not a vehicle of the Truth because these ideals lie behind any "Perfect State." This part ends with a prayer to God for help.

"The Vision of the Shepherds," following "The Summons," presents the shepherds in a conventional manner. They are poor and simple but are more modern than pastoral. "Although simpler than the complicated magi," remarks Hoggart, "they are shrewd enough to be ironical, in an appropriate conversational metre, about the status accorded to them by the powers of this world." Unlike the magi, the shepherds know only to keep the mechanism going and yet they too "know something will happen." They are being summoned as the Wisemen are. They say that in spite of poverty and hardship they don't despair. The shepherds in all their simplicity and faith get an assurance from the Chorus of Angels:

Unto you a Child,
A Son is given.
Praising, proclaiming
The ingression of Love,

Earth's darkness invents
The blaze of Heaven
And frigid silence
Meditates a song. (168)

Incidentally, this part effectively counters the criticism that Auden lacks sympathy for the common man. As Spears observes, "This section alone would be enough to refute those who say Auden lacks understanding of or sympathy with the common man; it is shrewd, amusing, and without condescension."[10]

The next section, "At the Manger," presents the conventional picture with Wise Men and the Shepherds. It begins with Mary's lullaby which means that her human flesh and maternal care can bring the Child anxiety, tears, sorrow and death. It is followed by the voices of the Wise Men and the Shepherds, the exceptional and the ordinary, who have been brought to the threshold of the truth by different paths. They have to undertake an endless journey and now they each cry for help—the first against intellectual pride and the second against sensual escapism. They conclude with an address to the Child in the person of that Love:

O Living Love, by your birth we are able
Not only, like the ox and ass of the stable,
To love with our live wills, but love,
Knowing are love.

The sixth section, "The Meditation of Simeon," reads as if it is Auden's statement of his belief. Just as Eliot wrote "A Song for Simeon" during his conversion, Auden too appears to have found an objective correlative in Simeon for his own: "The figure of Simeon is understandably attractive to writers whose convictions have traced a curve similar to that of Auden—he symbolizes the man to whom Truth came late, but with great consolation, and who thereupon gave praise."[11] Spears remarks that Simeon's statement "is probably the best brief exposition of Auden's religious position, or at least of its intellectual aspects."[12] Comparison between Eliot's Simeon and Auden's is inevitable. While Eliot's Simeon is old, tired, part Gerontion, part Tiresias, Auden's Simeon expresses himself energetically and idiomatically. Auden's Simeon speaks at length on the implications of the birth of Christ and his speech reflects the philosophy and theology of Kierkegaard.

"The Meditation" is about the philosophical meaning of the Incarnation. It has two parts—the first describes man's unavailing efforts to be self-sufficient; the second expresses the fullness of the answer in God. Simeon is presented as an earnest theologian who rationalizes his conversion and so his meditation becomes a sermon. His meditation epitomizes themes which were central to Auden's thought at this time. The foremost of these is man's self-deception that there are answers other than the religious to the Fall. Man convinces himself that the Fall did not really occur or that if it did occur it was by necessity or by accident. Man refuses to admit the existence of sin. Simeon says that only when man becomes conscious of his sinful nature can the word be made Flesh: "The word could not be made Flesh until men had reached a state of absolute contradiction between clarity and despair in which they would have no choice but either to accept absolutely or to reject absolutely." (181)

Simeon traces the events which occurred before man was in a position to accept Christ's Advent. He expresses the nature of God's achievement in His appearance on earth in the form of Christ:

> By the event of this birth the true significance of all other events is defined, for of every other occasion it can be said that it could have been different but of this birth it is the case that it could in no way be other than it is. And by the existence of this Child, the proper value of all other existences is given, for of every other creature it can be said that it has extrinsic importance but of this Child it is the case that He is in no sense a Symbol. (181)

The unique nature of incarnation and how it affected every one in his relationship with others is here underlined. Christ "is in no sense a Symbol"; He is real and His existence gives value to all others. Simeon then proceeds to clarify the distinction between sin and temptation: "for in Him we become fully conscious of Necessity as our freedom to be tempted, and of Freedom as our necessity to have faith." (182) The meaning of Time is illuminated "for the course of History is predictable in the degree to which all men love themselves, and spontaneous in the degree to which each man loves God and through Him his neighbour." (182) The elimination of the distinction between the ordinary and the exceptional is another consequence of the Incarnation: "disaster is not the impact of a curse upon a few great families, but issues continually from the hubris of every tainted will." (182) Furthermore,the Ridiculous is no longer confined to the Ugly "for since of themselves all men are without merit, all are ironically assisted to their comic bewilderment by the grace of God." (182) There is not a situation which is more or less interesting: "Every tea-table is a battlefield littered with old catastrophes and haunted by the vague ghosts of vast issues, every martyrdom an occasion for fly cracks and sententious oratory." (182-83) Simeon finally explains the metaphysical value of Trinity: "Because in Him the word is united to the Flesh . . . the One and the Many are simultaneously revealed as real." (183) The truth is indeed one but the possibilities of real knowledge are many. Simeon describes in a modern form of Dante's "In His will is our peace," the nature of grace, the achievement of which has become once again, through Christ, a possibility: "And because of His visitation, we may no longer desire God as if He were lacking: Our redemption is no longer a question of pursuit but of surrender to Him who is always and everywhere present. Therefore at every moment we pray that, following Him, we may depart from our anxiety into His Peace." (183-84)

If Simeon represents the Christian convert, Herod, in the next part, "the Massacre of the Innocents," represents the liberal intellectual championing the cause of reason. Herod's long outburst, a fusion of ancient and modern, involves a series of ironies resulting from the contrast between Herod's rationalism and Simeon's religious exposition. As Bahlke suggests:

> The position in the poem as a whole of Herod's soliloquy is determined by the level of irony which is to be evoked; it must

> follow Simeon's meditation so that Herod's argument will be undercut at every point by the reader's knowledge that he is seeing only a part of the situation. Although Herod foresees with terrifying accuracy some of the consequences of Christianity, he does not know, or will not accept, the truth which gives all his arguments a peripheral quality."

Herod's witty, amusing and highly persuasive arguments counter-balance Simeon's. He begins with a condemnation of the rumour of the Incarnation and says that it is a threat to the orderly rational world built by him. His long struggle to establish order and stamp out superstition are threatened by the rumour:

> And what, after all, is the whole Empire, with its few thousand square miles on which it is possible to lead the Rational Life, but a tiny path of light compared with those immense areas of barbaric night that surround it on all sides, that incoherent wilderness of rage and terror, where Mongolian idiots are regarded as sacred and mothers who give birth to twins are instantly put to death, where malaria is treated by yelling . . where it is firmly believed that the world was created by a giant with three heads or that the motions of the stars are controlled from the liver of a rogue elephant? (18)

In this contrast between Herod's kingdom with barbaric societies bordering it, there is the implicit suggestion that Christianity is just another form of superstition.

In spite of his constant efforts in the advancement of reason, Herod has noticed signs of man's interest in "the myth of divine origin" which is an easy kind of religion:

> So, with a bellow of rage, it (the public) kicks Poetry downstairs and sends for Prophecy." . . . The God I want and intend to get must be someone I can recognize immediately without having to wait and see what he says or does. There must be nothing in the least extraordinary about him. Produce him at once, please, I'm sick of waiting." (188)

Man turns from poetry to ask for a God who is not different from himself. Herod dismisses the prophecy concerning the divine origin. He predicts the consequences in terms, as Spears says, "sometimes recalling Yeats's play, *The Resurrection* and sometimes recalling Nietzsche."[14] Herod says that the replacement of reason by revelation means subjectivity taking the place of knowledge gained from science: "Reason will be replaced by Revelation. Instead of Rational Law, objective truths perceptible to any who will undergo the necessary intellectual discipline, and the same for all, knowledge will degenerate into a riot of subjective visions." (188) The Revelation will augment man's need for something visible to worship thus replacing idealism by materialism. The infinite mercy of God substitutes pity for justice: "The Rough Diamond, the Consumptive Whore, the bandit who is good to his mother, the epileptic girl who has a way with animals will be the heroes and heroines of the New Tragedy when the general, the statesman, and the philosopher have become the butt of every farce and satire." (189) Herod, being a proud rationalist, rejects a God who will sup people's initiative and self-respect: "Naturally this cannot be allowed to happen. Civilization must be saved even if this means sending for the military. . . . Why can't people be sensible? I don't want to be horrid. Why can't they see that the notion of a finite God is absurd?" (189) Herod is afraid of the emotional and subjective, the imaginative and the spiritual. The prophecy of the birth of the Child evidently annoys him. He refuses to believe it partly because if he accepts it as truth it means a great responsibility for him. It is unreasonable that a decision as to the existence of God is to be taken by him. As Spears puts it, Herod "refuses to go beyond the secular and rejects the existentialist Choice."[15] He despairs like a man who realizes that he can destroy God by not believing, like a man who has dreadful doubts but who cannot bring himself to believe without proof, and like a man clinging to reason alone but getting no final answer from it. Uneasily and self-pityingly, Herod concludes: "I 've tried to be good. I brush my teeth every night. I haven't had sex for a month. I object. I'm a liberal. I want everyone to be happy. I wish I had never been born." (190) The historical character of Herod has been changed into a humane, liberal intellectual. In fact, this part is very imaginative and, in terms of relevance to our own times, Herod's soliloquy is a great success/achievement. None disagrees with Fuller's comment when he says:

> What one admires about this part of the oratorio is that Auden has rejected the temptation to make Herod into the traditional raging tyrant. Herod is more effective for Auden's purposes, not as a Hitler, but as a representative of those attitudes which have no ultimate sanction against a Hitler. It is at this point (perhaps a little late) that the interest of the non-Christian is guaranteed.[16]

A more interesting and significant observation has been made by Bahlke that Auden has made Herod not only explore rational attitude toward Christianity but also consider some of the less fortunate consequences of Christianity:

> It should be clear that Herod's soliloquy is not only an exploration of the rational attitude toward Christianity and consequently a revelation of the sterile landscape and lives under its aegis, but also a consideration of some of the less fortunate consequences of Christianity. Auden has never ignored the existence of such consequences. In his introduction to the Greek Reader, for example, he points out that only a Christian society could have given rise to the Don Juan and Tristan Isolde myths, because they are negative responses to the imperatives involved in the acceptance of the religious sphere of existences.[17]

In a way Auden makes Herod express his own view that the truths of Christianity, when separated from their sacred sources, are likely to have a pernicious influence because they suppress the truth that romantic lovers are equally unhappy.

Herod's soliloquy is followed by Soldiers's speech characterized by callous brutality and cynical humour representing the perennial cruelty and evil of human nature. Rachel, Joseph's mother, weeps over the massacred innocents and says that "grinning dogs'' on the Left and ''sensible sheep, gazing up at a pride'' on the Right, meaning sensuality and proud reason are the two ways chosen by man. Between them is ''a lost child,'' the Son of God.

The final part of the oratorio, ''The Flight into Egypt,'' epitomizes the grief and the endless journeying of man. As Joseph and Mary undertake their journey through the desert, they hear the Voices of the Desert, which represent the temptations of the ''normal'' and particularly normal world. The desert through which the family passes is a symbol of lifeless decadence of modern society. In *The Enchanted Flood* (1950), Auden explains the symbolism of the Desert: ''it is the abode of those who reject or are rejected by the city, with the modern connotations of spiritual drouth, triviality, mechanization, and level uniformity. In 'The Shield of Achilles' and 'Plains' the Desert is the symbol of modern life at its worst.''[18] Joseph and Mary comment on life and observe that man is haunted by a sense of insecurity:

> Safe is Egypt we shall sigh
> For lost insecurity;
> Only when her terrors come
> Does our flesh feel quite at home. (194)

The recitative which follows is an interpretation of the Flight as a redemption of the past. The Holy Family of Joseph and Mary will

> Abscond with the Child to the place
> That their children dare not visit, to the time
> They do not care to remember; hide from our pride
> In our humiliation;
> Fly from our death with our new life. (194-95)

Once the Holy Family has left, the narrator appears to comment on the end of Christmas in modern life. It is a long speech in modern Idiom. It is at once amusing and profound. The Christmas season in modern times is described with great precision. The zeal and solemnity, a respectful homage, a sense of awe and reverence, a tribute to the great sacrifice, the joy of love which once marked the

Christmas have given place to a mere mechanical celebration confined to decorations and feasts:

> Now we must dismantle the tree,
> Putting the decorations back into their cardboard boxes—
> Some have got broken—and carrying them upto the attic.
> (195)

The chorus of daily life brings them back from the memories of the child.

> Once again
> As in previous years we have seen the actual Vision and failed
> To do more than entertain it as an agreeable,
> Possibility, once again we have sent Him away,
> Begging though to remain His disobedient servant,
> The Promising child who can not keep His word for long
> (195)

Man has a Vision of the divine event and all it implies, but painfully realizes his inadequacy to keep it alive all through the year. It is an ironic comment on man's failure to relive and experience Christ in everyday life. He thinks of the future, of the coming of Lent and Good Friday:

> The Christmas Feast is already a fading memory,
> And already the mind begins to be vaguely aware
> Of an unpleasant whiff of apprehension at the thought
> Of Lent and Good Friday. (195)

Man finds that to deal properly with this world and the present time is most difficult. To escape guilt and inhibit self-reflection, man is tempted to pray for temptation and suffering so that he may experience God's grace. They will come, but

> In the meantime
> There are bills to be paid, machines to keep in repair,

> Irregular verbs to learn, the Time Being to redeem
> From insignificance. (196)

"The Time Being," between Christmas and Good Friday, between the birth of Christ and the hope which that birth holds out to man, and His death, the sacrifice the knowledge of which man attempts to suppress is also the "years intervening between every man's birth and death, in which is held out to him the possibility of accepting his weaknesses and of entering that order which is the means of attaining a new relation to God." The narrator's speech ends, as Spears suggests, with a metaphor developed later in"Nones" and in the rest of "Horae Canonicae":

> The happy morning is over,
> The night of agony still to come; the time is noon;
> When the Spirit must practise his scales of rejoicing
> Without even a hostile audience, and the Soul endure
> A silence that is neither for nor against her faith
> That God's Will will be done, that, in spite of her prayers,
> God will cheat no one, not even the world of its triumph. (196)

The chorus with which the oratorio ends celebrates the transformation of the mundane by the Incarnation as "the Land of Unlikeness," "the Kingdom of Anxiety," "The World of the Flesh," where The Quester will achieve his fairy-tale wish. Thus Auden "with a cheerful disregard of historical nuance" makes *For the Time Being* "a vast historico-cultural fresco of the Nativity" treating "the contemporary world as another Roman empire at its last spiritual, gasp-thirst for the child."[19]

For the Time Being is undoubtedly concerned with the apprehension of the modern sensibility of the experiential and existential implications of the advent of Christ or the Incarnation for man's condition upon the earth which explains the use of parallelisms expressive of contemporary life and the introduction of various types of human character and facets of religious experience. It is, indeed, a remarkable attempt of literature to transfer theodicy into its own realm in order that the Man in relation to God, world and nature may be apprehended as an aesthetic phenomenon.

NOTES

1. Monroe K Spears quoting from Auden's letter to him as evidence says that the oratorio was written in 1941-42 and parts of it were published in periodicals. See *The Poetry of Auden*, pp. 205, 246n.
2. *For the Time Being* in *Collected Longer Poems* (London: Faber, 1968).
3. Monroe K Spears, p. 206.
4. Richard Hoggart, p. 183.
5. Gerald Nelson, *Changes of Heart: A Study of the Poetry of W.H. Auden, Perspectives in Criticism* (Berkeley: University of California Press, 1969), p. 62.
6. Hoggart, p. 185.
7. Nelson, pp. 66-67.
8. Spears, p. 210.
9. Hoggart, p. 188.
10. Spears, p. 212.
11. Hoggart, p. 189.
12. Spears, p. 213.
13. George W Bahlke, *The Later Auden: From "New Year Letter" to "About the House"* (New Brunswick, New Jersey: Rutgers University Press, 1970), p. 127.
14. Spears, p. 215.
15. *Loc. cit.*
16. John Fuller, p. 155.
17. Bahlke, p. 129.
18. Spears, p. 246.
19. Francois Duchene, p. 136.

The Sea and the Mirror: A Commentary on Shakespeare's *The Tempest*

Auden's *The Sea and the Mirror*[1] (1944) is highly complex in that it does not have a discernible form or structure as suggested by its sub-title, "Commentary on Shakespeare's *The Tempest,*" not to speak of its being symbolist in character. Moreover, it is in this work that Auden confronts the profound question of the relation of art to reality brought out by the title itself, the sea of life and the mirror of art. However, Auden does not explore this question in any conventional terms such as those related to mimetic or semiotic categories of interpretations. Nor does he concern himself with such questions as artist's attempt to aestheticize man's encounter with life. In choosing *The Tempest* as the point of departure for his dramatic discourse, Auden is able to frame the hermenuetics of question and answer which is at the heart of his "reading" of Shakespeare's play. As a result of this procedure as it were, a kind of tension ensues between the structural and structural-semiotic planes which accounts among other things for the realization of the dramatic and the poetic in *The Tempest.*

The Sea and the Mirror evokes a setting—that of a theatre which remains implied rather than overtly brought out. This in itself represents a novel experiment in the structuring of a dramatic work—an experiment that conforms to Auden's own view of man's relation to God and world which signals for him not a theodicy but a provocation. It is significant that the work starts with an address by the Stage Manager to the Critics of all people and ends with a speech echoed by the Prompter. This implies that Auden's principal concern is with representation of a closet drama which in the process of realization affords both a criticism and a description of the issues raised, issues such as those identifiable with the Kierkegaardian categories of the aesthetic, the ethical and the religious. It is difficult to identify the three divisions of *The Sea and the Mirror* with the Kierkegaardian categories if only for the reason that they are not sharply distinguished through the highlighting of the issues stemming from them within the respective sections of the work. But it is possible to suggest that the tripartite division is intended to explore the hermenuetic possibilities and determinations with which it seems instinct. It is interesting to observe that Auden does not project any materialistic dialectic which will require justification but focuses on the metaphysics of man's attempt or need to redeem himself in the eyes of his Creator or in terms of his best self ordained or warranted by his gifts and powers.

Like the long reflective poem *New Year Letter* with its meditations on literature, the War, politics, history, theology, philosophy, *The Sea and the Mirror* is primarily a meditation on art and life. Auden sets himself to do it by drawing on materials that already exist as a unity in the cultural consciousness. If the *New Testament* serves as a point of reference to *For the Time Being*, and Langland's *Piers Plowman* to *The Age of Anxiety*, Shakespeare's *Tempest* permits him to meditate and speculate on art and life, imagination and reality, Ariel and Caliban. The reliance on literary consciousness presents special difficulties and problems for readers. As Auden himself puts it: "The modern artist works with a consciousness of all the cultural productions, not only of the whole world of his own day, but also of the whole historical past."[2] Auden's method fortunately differs from that of others in that he accepts the literary and cultural consciousness whole-heartedly that the reader's approach to it is likely to be enhanced by his acquaintance with the play.

Auden's interest in *The Tempest* dates back to his school years marked by intellectual radicalism and Leftist political propaganda. Auden along with Christopher Isherwood, Edward Upward, C. Day Lewis, Stephen Spender and Rex Warner embodied their common beliefs and systems in the "Mortmere," a myth of their own. The Auden group derived and developed its myth partly from Marx and partly from the psychological theories of Freud, Jung, Homer Lane and Groddeck. *The Orators* embodies many of the group's interests, literary, non-literary, public and private sources. One of the systems that came in for strong criticism from the group is the honours system at Gresham School:

> In his final term at Gresham's, the summer of 1925, Wystan made his last appearance in the annual school play. It was *The Tempest.* He was determined to play Caliban, for he had firm views about the role's interpretation. Caliban's inheritance of the island on the departure of his master Prospero whom he loathed and feared was seen by Auden as an opportunity to make a protest against Gresham's honours system. He succeeded in getting the role, but whether he also succeeded in making his protest clear through his performance is by no means certain. The producer of the play was Wystan's housemaster whom he had cordially hated ever since the housemaster caught him writing a poem during prep, and sneered, "You shouldn't waste your sweetness on the desert air like this, Auden." Ten years later, Auden still could not think of this man without wishing him evil.[3]

The foregoing account goes to show Auden's deep hatred of academy presided over by teachers who sought to suppress the genuine instincts of their pupils. That he was determined to play Caliban is enough evidence of his understanding of that character.

Long after leaving Gresham's, Auden was still fond of discussing *The Tempest.* Discussing the contractual nature of master-servant relationship in literature in an essay "Balaam and His Ass," Auden underlines the Nature-Spirit dichotomy: "*The Tempest* seems to me a manichean work, not because it shows the relations of Nature to Spirit as one of conflict and hostility, which in fallen man it is, but because it puts the blame for this upon Nature and makes the Spirit innocent."[4] In "Music in Shakespeare," Auden says: "*The Tempest* is full of music of all kinds, yet it is not one of the plays in which in a symbolic sense, harmony and concord triumph over dissonant disorder."[5] Comparing the play with the three preceding romantic comedies *Pericles, Cymbeline* and *The*

Winter's Tale, Auden observes that while the earthly music in *The Tempest* is reflective of heavenly music, in the others it is sour. It appears as though this play of Shakespeare was in Auden's consciousness throughout his life.

The sea and sea voyage in Shakespeare's last plays symbolizing purgatorial suffering leading to the world of music and marriage have hermenuetic possibilities. That Auden was fully aware of the possibilities that *The Tempest* held out is beyond doubt: "*The Tempest* provides Auden with a widely known situation that can help particularize the terms of his own analysis; it also frees him from the necessity of developing his own specific characters. If Auden's use of Shakespeare makes *The Sea and the Mirror* less than self-sufficent as a work of art, the price for such a brilliance is small."[6] In fact, Auden's use of Shakespeare's play makes it richer than ever and by showing its complex symbolic structure, he is crediting himself and his own play. Commenting on the appropriateness of the choice of Shakespeare's play, Bahlke observes: "The choice of *The Tempest* as a symbolic basis for Auden's poem is appropriate because the world of that play is one of reconciliation and forgiveness; it is a world in which Prospero abjures his art, not because it has no value in itself, but because it has fulfilled his purpose through effecting a reconciliation between those who were divided from one another by hatred, pride and inadequate love."[7] Although Auden accepts Shakespeare's play as a symbolic basis, he seems to question several of the play's assumptions. He worked on the poem so carefully that the notebook he used contains everything from first tentative lists of characters and verse forms to much of the finished work: "This manuscript would provide rich material for a study of the composition; it effectively gives the lie to any notion that Auden is a careless writer who never blots a line, for it shows him both revising painstakingly and minutely and often completely rewriting passages in a different form or style."[8]

The Sea and the Mirror has a tripartite structure. It is, as Edward Callan suggests, "arranged like a triptych with separate panels for the artist, the work of art, and the audience." Part One, "Prospero to Ariel," is a dramatic monologue in three parts marked by interpolated lyrics; Part Two, "The Supporting Cast *Sotto*

Voce," is a cycle of lyrical monologues spoken by Ferdinand, Stephano, Gonzalo, Adrian, Francisco, Alonso and Miranda with interruptions of Antonio. Part Three, "Caliban to the Audience," is a clever address in which Caliban, speaking to and for the audience discusses art and life. The "Preface" spoken by the "Stage Manager to the Critics," and the "Postscript" from Ariel to Caliban round out the work. "The 'Preface' addressed to the critics may be, in part, an ironic reminder that the three panels in the triptych correspond to *source, form and end*—the three categories of questions that critics perennially ask of art."[9] The triptych metaphor appropriately describes the elegant formal structure of the work. The differentiating verse forms given to each character give formal unity in diversity within the tripartite framework.

The Sea and the Mirror begins where *The Tempest* ends. Shakespeare's play closes with Prospero's "Epilogue" which raises serious questions about the nature of art. It may be said that *The Sea* is a commentary on the four lines of Prospero's epilogue:

> Now I want
> Spirits to enforce, art to enchant;
> And my ending is despair
> Unless I be relieved by prayer.

Prospero who might be Shakespeare himself playing the triple role of stage-manager, playwright and actor, moves away from the play presenting a world of characters outside himself that at the same time embody the conflicts and harmonies of a single consciousness. In the same way, Auden offers a commentary on *The Tempest* and at the same time uses the characters and experiences of the play for his material. According to Callan, the "compelling reason for choosing the end of *The Tempest* as a point of departure may have been the implication in Prospero's 'Epilogue' (sometimes read as an abjuration of art) that the artistic life could be incompatible with ethical or spiritual values. . . . Auden's point of departure, then, suggests that concern of an artist for the ultimate value of his work which troubled Chaucer, Tolstoy, and (in some interpretations of *The Tempest*) Shakespeare. By presenting his solution in the form of a work of art, Auden undercuts the 'dilemma'; for, while he rejects Romanticism's special stress on the autonomy of the imagination, he reaffirms the value of art in this technically brilliant work prodigal with apt verse-forms.''[10]

The ''Preface'' of the Stage Manager to the Critics raises the problem of art versus reality. With his familiarity with the world of art, of illusion, the Stage Manager discourses to the Critics on the limits of art and the difference from life. In the first stanza, the Stage Manager speaks of the effects on the spectators of illusions which he manipulates: while the innocent children accept the aesthetic pretence as essentially play, the ''aged catch their breath,'' since terror and death are part of their consciousness and reality. In the second stanza, the Stage Manager ironically suggests that rational explanations fail to account for the surprises of existence. The rational order cannot explain the irrational. Art, being essentially human, can at best evoke emotions from a conjured spectacle. In the third stanza, he says that ''art has a relationship to life: it represents the *agony* in the ideal form; but goes on to question the practical effectiveness of art in the real struggle—The existential *agon*.''[11]:

> but how
> Shall we satisfy when we meet,
> Between Shall-I and I-Will,
> The lion's mouth whose hunger
> No metaphors can fill?[12] (203)

In the last stanza a clear demarcation between the world of reality and the world of illusion is made. The people represented in art are insubstantial. The Stage Manager echoes Hamlet and Lear at the close of his speech suggesting that Shakespeare was aware of this limitation of art:

> All the rest is silence
> On the other side of the wall;
> And the silence ripens,
> And the ripeness all. (202)

Commenting on the Shakespearean echoes in the "Preface," McDowell observes:

> This passage reveals Auden's skill in making fresh poetry from familiar Shakespearean phrases. The last four lines, moreover, convey an acceptance and a reconciliation, linked with Ariel's wisdom in the postscript. There Ariel, who is the artistic impulse in essence, wants Caliban as he is, and welcomes "reality," epitomized in Caliban, no matter how gross and grotesque. The ripeness is all, both for Ariel who welcomes Caliban's "drab mortality" and for Caliban, who, in his long prose speech, disparages the production he has just witnessed and by implication the whole human performance, but who still perceives through it intimations of the "Wholly Other Life."[13]

In "Prospero to Ariel," Prospero bids farewell to Ariel preparing himself to leave the enchanted island. It is the "resigning thoughts" of a creative artist who has in the past relied wholly on imagination and who has now come to realize the inadequacies of aesthetic life. Prospero is, in Kierkegaardian terms, renouncing the aesthetic for the religious. He is discovering that "art is not substitute for religion even for the artist, whose art gives him no special privileges from the religious standpoint."[14]

Prospero's reflections on the past and the present and his vision of the future are all embodied here. His consciousness telescopes various periods of his life including the future. This part of the poem could be read as the career of a man with and without the faculty of imagination. Prospero describes his situation, a situation that might be true of any artist who sees the limitation of his art. Now he is aware of his double destiny as retired artist and emergent human being. In his role of an emergent human being, he wants to recover his humanity subverted under magic robes but is unwilling to give up his magician's reputation. As Blair puts it: "The master of the power to enchant can see himself clearly only when he gives up his dependence on the Ariel of the imagination. Heretofore Ariel has been kept busy magically remaking the real world to conform to his master's idea of the way things should be. Now Prospero sees what the freely acting imagination can show him: 'All we are not stares back at what we are.' Living on without his familiar imagination is bound to be hard.''[15]

In Section II, Prospero's reflections on art continue but there is a rigorous self-examination. He says that art takes us into an ideal realm of order but it may fail us in acquiring a knowledge of undistorted reality. Prospero realizes the misconception that the harmonies of art are easily attained in life. He rebukes himself for forgetting the two promises he had made to himself: "To hate nothing and to ask nothing for its love." (206) It is his aesthetic withdrawal which encouraged Antonio into evil resulting in mutual hatred. Again, it is "a wish/for absolute devotion" that made Prospero mould Caliban. Prospero broke both of these promises placing himself not as an isolated man among men but as an isolated man above men. He exchanged life for the "mirror of art," believing that in this mirror he would see things idealized, see himself as he wished to be. But when he looked into the mirror of Ariel's "calm eyes," he saw Caliban and realized that, far from getting an idealized picture from the mirror, "All we are not stares back at what we are." Prospero owns his failure to "hate nothing and to ask nothing for its love," (206) but his failure with Caliban annoys him more because it undermines his success over all other men:

> But Caliban remains my impervious disgrace.
> We did it, Ariel, between us; result—his wreck
> That sprawls in the weeds and will not be repaired.
> My dignity discouraged by a pupil's curse,
> I shall go knowing and incompetent into my grave. (206-7)

Commenting on Prospero's self-mockery, McDowell observes:

> The rejection of Caliban is fateful for Prospero because he evades the truth about himself, because he will not recognize the ugly and the grotesque, and because he lacks the imagination to understand a sinister being he had himself in part

engendered. In the Kierkegaardian sense, Prospero has insight at the aesthetic and moral levels, but lacks insight at the religious. Intellectually to be admired, Prospero in Auden's view lacks the radical charity—or Agape—discernible at times even in reprobates like Falstaff: "Agape requires that we love our enemies, do good to those that hate us, and forgive those who injure us, and this command is unconditional." The formidable Prospero pays lip service to Agape, but does not "unconditionally" embrace it. As Auden says in another connection, "Prospero forgiving is more the contemptuous pardon of a man who knows he has his enemies completely at the mercy than a heartfelt reconciliation."[16]

In Section III of "Prospero to Ariel," Prospero says that he got over his hang over and hang up but feels so peculiar as if he had been drunk since he was born and suddenly now is "cold sober": "With all my unanswered wishes and unwashed days/stacked up all round my life." He had been on some tremendous journey "sketching imaginary landscapes, chasms and cities,/Cold Walls, hot spaces, wild mouths, defeated backs,/Jotting down fictional notes on secrets overheard/In theatres and privies, banks and mountain inns." (208) He now comes to feel that the real journey of life begins not with the wish or the mirror, but with the silence of the self. Old age with the attendant misfortunes makes him alive to the stark and naked realities of life. "Alone and on foot, without a cent in my pocket," Prospero visualizes his life against a universe where time is not foreshortened. His journey from now on is going to be a religious one in which he will no longer be interesting, but will appear perfectly ordinary. He will not be able to speak, but must "learn to suffer/without saying something ironic or funny/On suffering?" (209) If he is fortunate, he may learn before he dies "The difference between moonlight and daylight."

Part II of *The Sea*, "The Supporting Cast, *Sotto Voce*" presents the remaining characters in Shakespeare's *The Tempest*, Caliban and Ariel excepted. Prospero's magic had a benevolent impact on them and all of them had undergone a sea-change. Auden's Prospero (in Part I) has spoken of "The extravagant children, who lately swaggered/Out of the sea like gods, have, I think, been soundly hunted/By their own devils into their human selves." (207) Antonio, the wicked usurper, however, remains outside the magic circle challenging Prospero and his art. His intransigence and refractoriness raise the philosophical question of human perfectibility and the prevalence and unsubjugation of evil in the world. Shakespeare's remarks on nature on which nurture cannot stick echoes Plato's "moral depravity." Calvin's dogma concerning the fallen condition of man, and Melville's vision of evil help us to understand Auden's Antonio. Antonio takes an ironic view of all characters, their metamorphoses, "As all the Pigs have twined back into men, " and the contrived happy ending. He makes it impossible for Prospero to renounce his magic by refusing to submit to it: "As long as I choose/To wear my fashion, whatever you wear/Is a magic robe; while I stand outside/Your circle, the will to charm is still there." (212) Unlike the stand-aloofishness in *The Tempest*, Antonio in *The Sea* is quite obtrusive. He dominates Part II with his speech and his "refrain ironically dominates the whole section in its expression of his unregenerate will, represents man's freedom to create the disorder which exists for art to make sense of."[17] As each character speaks, with his mocking chorus Antonio reveals the changes in his personality that Prospero's art has effected.

Antonio dominates not only this part but the poem as a whole. Unreconciled figure that he is, he threatens the hard-won peace others attained: "Antonio will prevent Prospero from attaining, first, pure "Being" and, secondly a perfect grouping of human beings, whereby the harmonies of art might be approximated in life. Antonio's is the motiveless malignity in the background that bides its time to destroy because it must. Antonio will constantly threaten the serenity of Prospero and tempt him to resurrect his wand he has broken and the books he has destroyed."[18] Auden's Antonio parallels Shakespeare's Iago and Melville's Claggart, to cite but a few, in unregenerate will and cynicism. Iago's "I am not what I am" is matched by Antonio's impudent utterance: "I am I, Antonio,/By choice myself alone." (212) Strong enough not to need art as fantasy and being "the permanent doubter and disbeliever, unsubmissive of will and proud of intellect, arrogant, cynical, non-conforming, efficient, individualistic," he dismisses it as "the seed of the man of power and the spiritual barbarian."[19]

Antonio belongs to the category of demonic heroes who are religious heroes turned upside down, defiant ones who assert their freedom by disobeying all commands. He is thus a negative religious hero who may be grouped with Faust, Don Juan, Captain Ahab, all of whom end in despair. An embodiment of evil, he is a force to reckon with but stands ignored until such time as his disastrous entrenchment is felt. He equals Prospero in toughness of fibre and strength of purpose. He seems to be waiting for an opportunity to destroy and humiliate his brother spiritually just as he wrenched the dukedom from him earlier. In "An absolute passion of aversion and hatred"[20] he is the devil, the absolute villain like Iago or Claggart. Auden by contrasting Antonio and Prospero seems to make a value judgment on their stances and indirectly on the value of art and reality. The movement of Prospero from the world of art, his casting aside of the manipulated stuff is of extreme importance. It is a progress from the aesthetic and ethical to the religious.

While Antonio speaks cynically of the division between others and himself, between the forces of order and disorder, Ferdinand envisions the principle of love which brings him closer to Miranda. Since he is a romantic lover, he is given Petrarchan sonnet which begins with Ferdinand's awakening to sensual awareness of Miranda, first as an object and then as a person—the "Dear other" of his consciousness:

> Within the limits of this sonnet Auden has presented in miniature much of the total theme of *The Sea and the Mirror*. In contrast to Antonio's negative self-love, which uses the imagination for vengeance, Ferdinand's "Other-directed" love makes right use of the imaginative faculty through which he recognizes the analogous relationship between the natural and the spiritual. Antonio, in mocking Ferdinand's love, does not see beyond the level of *Eros*.[21]

Ferdinand's love is not sensual only: "I would smile at no other promise than touch, taste, sight" but "another tenderness," a light which enables the lovers to possess "The Right Required Time, the Real Right Place, O Light." Ferdinand grasps agape through eros.

Stephano's ballad with its refrain, "A lost thing looks for a lost name," addressed to his belly, shows him as a man who has given himself up. His belly, representative of his body and heavy with drink, has become through "humble pie and swallowed pride" "wise nanny" behind whose "skirts your son must hide." (213) He tries to know himself with the help of alcohol because it dispels melancholy ("The high play better than the blue") and gives the illusion of a unity of mind and body although "The will of one by being two/At every moment is denied." (214)

Gonzalo looks back at the island "where/All our loves were altered." He remembers the prediction he had made and which has now come true. He was fond of his booming eloquence but now he feels that he should have "trusted the Absurd." In an obvious reference to Ariel's song in *The Tempest* (Act II, Scene i), he says that he ought to have reproduced it. On the other hand, he had frozen "Vision into an idea" through "Doubt and insufficient love" and "made the song/sound ridiculous and wrong." Now like "a bell," he is ready to express the divine will. The couplet of Adrian and Francisco embodies their confusion and its brevity represents the vacuity of mind of the speakers. It has been said that the couplet of Adrian and Francisco "is surrealistically smart, presumably to suggest their precosity and sophistication." Adrian and Francisco seem to realize the falsity of their erstwhile country life. They have been shown a sounder way of life and they are now to train themselves to follow it.

Alonso, the foremost among the reconciled men, "now ready to welcome/Death, but rejoicing in a new love,/A new peace, having heard the solemn music and seen the statue move/To forgive our illusion," (219) addresses his son Ferdinand, who is soon ascending the throne majestically, warning him against the pitfalls in his journey of kingship. Subtle in ideas, informal in tone, and solemn in sentiment, Alonso's speech presents a dual perspective and accounts for a continuous development. He begins by drawing

Ferdinand's attention to the world of objects. Discordant and sinister images "the water where fish/see sceptres descending," "the sands where a crown/Has the status of a broken down/Sofa or mutilated statue" (216-17) convey the unpredictable in royal existence. The sea and the desert symbolize duality of existence, physical and spiritual, life and death, matter and mind.[22] Man is caught between these extremes of duality—the sea and the desert, ice and fire.

Alonso draws Ferdinand's attention to "others" who tactfully keep the king in ignorance of "the shark and the octopus." The hypocritical courtiers give a false impression of harmony and order. Describing the unconscious and conscious choice and hope, Alonso asks the Prince to beware of the ornate mirror which might entangle him in the sea or leave him undressed in a desert. Between these two extremes, the "way of Justice is a tightrope." The temptations from the sea, "a night/where all flesh had peace," and from the desert, "a brilliant void/where his mind could be perfectly clear/And all his limitations destroyed." (218) To become a victim of either of these temptations is "To join all the unjust kings." Presenting the political world, Alonso warns Ferdinand of the difficulty of holding to the way of justice, avoiding both the "watery vagueness" and the "triviality of the sand," steering between "loose craving" and "sharp aversion," "aimless jelly" and "paralyzed bone" remembering "that the fire and the ice/Are never more than one step away/From the temperate city." (218-19)

Towards the end, Alonso says that if Ferdinand were to lose his kingship like himself he should "praise the scorching rocks/For the desiccation of your lust" and "Thank the bitter treatment of the tide/For its dissolution of your pride" so that "the whirlwind may arrange your will/And the deluge release it." (219) He will then find the "spring in the desert the fruitful/Island in the sea, where flesh and mind/Are delivered from mistrust." (219) The images in the final stanza of Alonso's letter symbolize harmony in the physical world—in the universe, the natural world and the king. This earthly harmony mirrors an analogous order in the world after death—a reality to which art has opened Alonso's eyes "having heard the solemn/Music strike and seen the statue move/To forgive our illusion." As Edward Callan observes, "Clearly, Alonso's letter contains one of the several expressions in *The Sea and the Mirror* of the positive value of Art."[23] As we have noticed in the foregoing, the two major symbols in Alonso's speech are the sea associated with the flesh, the senses, potentiality, and subjectivity, and the desert associated with the mind, abstraction, the temptation to ignore the limitations of the human creature. Auden suggests that by "balancing one against the other, and allowing each to purge the characteristic vice of the other—the desert drying up lust, the sea dissolving pride—can the two be reconciled and the oasis in the desert or island in the sea be found."[24]

The Master and the Boatswain sing an Audenesque ballad, an example of the concentration and aptness of the poetry in *The Sea*, drawing on Stephano's song in *The Tempest*. It pictures the loneliness and hopelessness of the sailors beneath the sensuality and debauchery. The sailors do come to terms with life of the sea.

Sebastian who dreamt of killing Alonso is happy that he has been exposed and is glad to realize that after all Love exists. He is anxious and joyous and for the first time he is free from anxiety: "I smile because I tremble, glad today/To be ashamed, not anxious, not a dream." He is no longer a negative personality even though his nature has been revealed in its nakedness: "In dreams all sins are easy, but by day/It is defeat gives proof we are alive;/ The sword we suffer is the guarded crown." Repenting his frustrated attempts to seize power and to plot his brother's death, Sebastian seems to define the spirit of negation, its easy assumption of power and its rejection of traditional ethics. He now accepts Prospero's world of co-inherence.

Trinculo, "the cold clown" "whose head is in the clouds" had "warmed" "Mechanic, merchant, King" and believed that he "never can get down." Now he becomes aware of his solitude and the inadequacy of his jests to reach "that solid world":

> A terror shakes my tree
> A flock of words fly out,
> Whereat a laughter shakes
> The busy and devout.

Wild images, come down
Out of your freezing sky,
That I, like shorter men,
May get my joke and die. (223-24)

Trinculo discovers that he is in despair and that his existence bears little relationship to his real self.

Part II of *The Sea* ends with Miranda's villanelle echoing Ferdinand's uniqueness of his love for her although her love is very much narrower than his. She recalls her past remembering it as a dream world with fairy-tale characters Caliban, Sycorax, Gonzalo and Ferdinand. In her naivety, she seems to imagine that her love will be permanent like "the high green hill (which) sits always by the sea." The line in her villanelle, "My Dear One is mine as mirrors are lonely," suggests varied meanings. It might be that "Ferdinand's eyes are more attractive mirrors for her, so that her looking-glass will no longer reflect her image, and was even lonely when she used it, for it could not see itself in her eyes as Ferdinand can."[25] Or it might suggest "not only the egotism of mirror-gazing but also the mirror which art holds upto nature."[26] Though several critics called it a "lovely" line, it remains an example of Auden's "tendency towards impressive vagueness, even towards a triteness or woolliness, of metaphor and simile."[27]

Part III, "Caliban to the Audience," a long symposium on the relationship between art and life, illusion and reality, seems patterned on the classical pattern of oration, with a prologue in which Caliban echoes audience's poser to the dramatist, the author of *The Tempest*, concerning the unsubjugated Caliban; an argument where Caliban speaks for Shakespeare to the promising artist; and a pre-oration where Caliban describes the roles of himself and Ariel in life. The Jamesian involuted prose style permits an ironical double focus Caliban desperately looks for. As Edward Callan observes:

> At its simplest, the framework of "Caliban to the Audience" is an elaboration of Auden's favourite ironic device of double focus: the dialectical opposition of ideas exemplified by such

essays as "Jehovah Housman and Satan Housman," "The Public vs. the Late Mr. William Butler Yeats," and "Two Sides to a Thorny Problem: Exploring Below the Surface of Shakespeare's *Merchant*." Henry James, whose work Auden greatly admires, uses a somewhat similar many-sided approach—comparable to a debate or symposium—which Auden considers valuable to modern man in his quest for truth.[28]

The dialectical nature of Caliban's "long-winded disquisition explains much of Auden's technique in verse of making opposites debate against each other. This device is employed in *The Dyer's Hand* in such discussions as demonic hero and the religious hero. Opinions vary from critic to critic and sometimes differ radically from one to another on this dialectic of Caliban. Joseph Warren Beach, whose primary concern is with Auden's revisions and alterations of his poems, dismisses Caliban's speech in these words: "More than half of *The Sea and the Mirror* (Caliban to the Audience) is a long-winded disquisition in prose on (as I understand it) literary-art-in-an-age-of-naturalistic-unbelief. It is in effect a clever but tiresome parody of the style of Henry James in his famous Prefaces."[29] If Beach finds Caliban's speech "a clever but tiresome parody," Barbara Everett describes it as "a small masterpiece, one of the funniest, cleverest, and most fundamentally tough paradoxically serious things Auden has ever produced:

> Caliban's speech is not an autonomous entity, but a piece of criticism; it forms an extraordinary meeting-point for the aesthetic that, Auden seems by it to suggest, was shared by the late work of two apparently diverse masters, Shakespeare and James; and it accepts that aesthetic as its own in interpreting life. Thus, the reader is likely to need not only a familiarity with and love of both *The Tempest* and James's later work, but a readiness to agree that Auden's critique of both is true or at least feasible; a readiness, moreover, to agree that this desired vision is in itself a possible insight into existence. To put at its simplest, the reader has, when Caliban looms into

view and opens his mouth to let loose the familiar unending and tortuous cadences, to be delighted by a triumphant critical metaphor: that the Ariel-haunted yet grossly and terribly physical monster, Caliban, is a perfect image of the lumbering and sweating delicacies, the deep-breathed and powerful and grotesque syntactical structures, weighed down with obstinately physical images, that emerge into a lucid simplicity of loving vision, in James's last novels. More than this: he has to agree that the two fused together create also another image, an image of interdependence of those two familiar contradictions, Art and Reality; and that the play of Ariel and Caliban, of what we perceive confusedly as art and reality, is itself a final expressive image of a divine world behind the scenes, where there is no division between the imagination and the real, between dramatist and play, between Creator and created. . . . One of the most delightful things Auden has ever done, carrying the assurance and freedom born of the happy discovery of a new means of communication, a new "fabulous country" where the poet can momentarily feel at home and at ease.[30]

Richard Hoggart finds Caliban's "dazzling" prose address heavily weighted with material and extravagant with metaphor and, therefore, makes the structure "lopsided." But he thinks Auden's change to prose "justifiable" because he had so much to say on themes, because Henry James's later prose—"its ability to express nuances, to condition, to present involved and highly qualified ideas—are exactly what Auden needs." Further, he says: "It is true that poetry—assuming a sensitive reader—can do all this more immediately but Caliban is addressing representatives of the unpoetic world. He does so in a manner they will recognize; he is confident, ironic, fluent and happily conversational."[31]

Caliban puts on three different masks. First, he wears a mask to pose the audience's questions to Shakespeare; second, to address the budding artist on behalf of Shakespeare; and finally on his own and Ariel's behalf. In *The Tempest,* Caliban relates to Stephano and Trinculo how Prospero employs magical art to torment him taking advantage of his gross ignorance. In *The Sea and the Mirror,* Caliban takes up the same argument and seems to question the dramatist's exploitation of the ignorance of the audience. Thus, Caliban in Auden's play is an extension of his prototype in Shakespeare, the difference being that while Shakespeare's Caliban is an epitome of brutal barbarity and unfeeling savageness, Auden's Caliban appears in the garb of a drama critic. If, as Nicholas Rowe observes, Shakespeare "had not only found out a new character in his Caliban, but had also adapted a new manner of language for that character,"[32] Auden too might be said to have devised and adapted a new manner of language for that character.

Caliban justifies, at the outset, his taking the curtain call instead of "so good, so great, so dead author" saying that he is "the begged question you would speak to him about." (225) He echoes the spectators's complaint that Shakespeare's "Epilogue" to *The Tempest* has destroyed the pleasant illusion of the play-world by releasing Caliban into the domain of imagination and Ariel into Caliban's. They wish to preserve the distinction between Art and Life. So Caliban voicing audience's annoyance in a tone of injured complaint, points out to Shakespeare his offence against decorum:

> How could you, you who are one of the oldest habitue's at these delightful functions, one, possibly the closest, of her trusted inner circle, how could you be guilty of the incredible unpardonable treachery of bringing along the one creature, as you above all men must have known, whom she cannot and will not under any circumstances stand, the solitary exception she is not any hour of the day or night at home to, the unique case that her attendant spirits have absolute instructions never, neither at the front door nor at the back, to admit? (227)

The English Muse is a society mistress for whom purity of genre or purity of style, classical unities do not matter, who has the power to combine and happily contrast social and moral problems unapproached and unattempted by the Greek or French dramatists, Caliban says that English drama "is the mixed perfected brew." Everything is under the Muse's command. All kinds of men are found and there is no segregation of the rich from the poor and the wise from the foolish. The spectators have got used to the "gracious goddess" and her ways and are willing to suspend their disbelief. They don't question the conjured world, its contrived situation and counterfeit resolutions. Everything is agreeable to them.

The English Muse admits every kind of being into her abode but "she cannot conceivably tolerate in her presence the represented principle of not sympathizing, not associating, not amusing, the only child of her Awful Enemy, the rival whose real name she will never sully her lips with—'that envious witch' is sign sufficient—who does not rule but defiantly is the unrectored chaos," Caliban. (227) Shakespeare committed an offence against decorum by letting loose the "unrectored chaos" into the world of harmony and order. The world of Art is one of freedom without anxiety, of "the perfectly tidiable case of disorder, the beautiful and serious problem exquisitely set without a single superfluous datum and insoluble with less." (229) To introduce Caliban, the symbol of reality, one of the stubbornly untransformable facts of actual existence, into this world is unforgivable. The audience insists that they are well aware that art is not life. They value art since it provides a totally free escape from the unpleasantness of actual life. They want to be charmed by the Muse:

> For we, after all—you cannot have forgotten this—are strangers to her (The Muse). We have never claimed her acquaintance, knowing as well as she that we do not and never could belong on her side of the curtain. All we have ever asked for is that for a few hours the curtain should be left undrawn, so as to allow our humble ragged selves the privilege of craning and gaping at the splendid goings-on inside. (228)

The audience insist on the division between the mirror world of art and the chaos of life. They fear that their beloved author, who has entertained them often, may have done more than simply shatter the illusion of the art world. In life, Caliban and Sycorax appear as Cupid and Venus: "the rude august elated archer of our heaven, the darling son of Her who, in her right milieu, is certainly no witch but the most sensible of all her Gods . . . our great white Queen of Love herself." (233) This confusion of realms may lead, the spectators think, to worse consequences:

> Is it possible that, not content with inveigling Caliban into Ariel's Kingdom, you have also let loose Ariel in Caliban's? We note with alarm that when the other members of the final tableau were dismissed, He was not returned to His arboreal confinement as He should have been. Where is he now? For if the intrusion of the real has disconcerted and incommoded the poetic, that is a mere bagatelle compared to the damage which the poetic would inflict if it ever succeeded intruding upon the real. We want no Ariel here, breaking down our picket fences in the name of fraternity, seducing our wives in the name of romance, and robbing us of our sacred pecuniary deposits in the name of justice. (233-34)

Having spoken on audience's behalf, Caliban now delivers a special message from Shakespeare to "any gay apprentice in the magical art who may have chosen this specimen of the prestidigitatory genus to study this evening in the hope of grasping more clearly just how the artistic contraption works." It is as much about the artist's hopes and fears as about the artist as a citizen. For the young artist Ariel, the creative imagination, is a faithful servant at first:

> He does come when you call. He does tell you all the gossip. He overhears on the stairs, all the goings-on. He observes through the keyhole; He really is willing to arrange anything you care to ask for, and you are rapidly finding out the right orders to give—who should be killed in the hunting accident, which couple to send into the cast-iron shelter, what scent will arouse a Norwegian engineer, how to get the young hero from the country lawyer's office to the Princess' reception, when to mislay the letter, where the cabinet minister should be reminded of his mother, why the dishonest valet must be a martyr to indigestion but immune from the common cold.

(235)

Throughout this section, Caliban sounds ironical pulling the rug from the artist's feet. The phrase "conjuror's profession," like "artistic verbal contraption," is not a neutral term. He is warning the artist against the temptations of Ariel. Once he has become a victim, he cannot wriggle himself out of the snare. Although he gains in self confidence, he moves away from the "howling merchants and transacting multitudes." Soon he learns the tricks of the trade: to contrive dramatic situations, to rouse expectations in the spectators, to resolve tangled relationships, to bring in deux ex machina etc. The partnership is a brilliant success. By and by, the artist's infinite conceptual appetite is sustained by vivid concrete experience. Initial wonder becomes an economic habit. Cocksureness becomes second nature. Nothing escapes. "No perception however *petite*, no notion however subtle, escapes your attention or baffles your understanding." (235)

However, the initial co-operation and co-ordination between the artist and the imagination suffers a setback as Ariel withdraws his power only to bestow it on other victims: "So it goes on from exasperated bad to desperate worst until you realize in despair that there is nothing for it but you two to part." In the inexplicable inarticulate condition, the artist tries to break loose from Ariel but realizes it an impossibility. Ariel refuses to go. The artist now glares into his "unblinking eyes" to find to his great amazement not what he had always seen "but a gibbering fist-clenched creature," Caliban. Caliban accuses the artist of not only indifference to him but charges him with escapist fancies. If the artist had allowed freedom for himself, freedom to live a sensual life, an unfettered and unchecked freewheeling way to disorder, he would have, nevertheless, come by "the bumpy third-class road of guilt and remorse smack into that very same truth." In this address the potential artist is warned that he is subject to a temptation similar to the audience's. He will want to believe that he can be the ideally imaginative Ariel to the exclusion of his grosser self, his Caliban of the body. The prospective artist must learn, as did Prospero, that he has a sea life to lead which is not "amenable to magic."

In the final section, Caliban chooses for his theme himself and Ariel. Moments ago, he spoke to the artists about his unignorable presence. Now he speaks to the audience about the choices they have to make in life. He begins by praising them for having taken the first step beyond a childish identification of art and life. They can now distinguish between the real and the imagined, Caliban with his "reiterated affirmation of what their furnished circumstances categorically are," and Ariel with "his successive propositions as to everything else they conditionally might be." Ariel and Caliban are involved in a tension since the former judges the latter by his standards. Human beings try to avoid the tension by turning to either of them. Using the metaphor of Journey, Caliban suggests that the ordinary and the exceptional are on a voyage across the sea in which most of the travellers will want to remain at the main depot, "the grandly Average Place" because it is more comfortable to stay on in the "land of habit." The Journey here "corresponds to Prospero's; its goal is knowledge of the self, and through the self, of one's relation to God."[33]

The ordinary man, says Caliban, asks to be taken to the days of his childhood. He has "never felt really well in this climate of distinct ideas" and he longs for a liberal condition and, once he achieves it, finds himself in a meaningless and thoroughly secular world far different from what he hoped to return to. The exceptional man, on the other hand, wants to transcend this particularized life, leap into a world of complete abstractions where man is free from necessity and has power without knowledge. In such a condition, one no longer relates events to their causes or to purposes beyond themselves: instead, "any sense of direction, any knowledge of where on earth one has come from or where on earth one is going to is completely absent." In summary, the two ways, of the ordinary and of the exceptional, use these primary routes man pursues. The ordinary goes to Caliban for help to escape into the world of his childhood, which he supposes to be real, only to find that it is very different from what he set out to recover. The exceptional asks Ariel, the power of the creative imagination, to take him into the unconditioned world he seeks. "The consequences of putting either Caliban or Ariel in charge," as Spears observes, "are vividly portrayed in symbolic fantasies that are fascinating, infinitely suggestive, and impossible to paraphrase.''[34] Those who seek Caliban ask him to take them to the lost Eden of childhood. But, Caliban admits, he cannot transport them to any such Eden ''which your memory necessarily but falsely conceives of as the ultimately liberal condition,'' but only to that state as it really is, a desolate and indifferent scene ''where Liberty stands with her hands behind her back, not caring, not minding *anything*.'' Caliban concludes in terms, as Spears says, that parody those of atheistic existentialism, ''your existence is indeed free at last to choose its own meaning, that is, to plunge headlong into despair and fall through silence fathomless and dry, all fact your single drop, all value your pure alas.''

Those who choose Ariel for their master are no better or happier. These ''important persons at the top of the ladder, exhausted lions of the season, local authorities with their tense tired faces, elderly hermits of both sexes living gloomily in the delta of a great fortune'' surrender to Caliban's ''spiritual colleague'' in the hope of escaping the mess of life. Ariel carries them into a ''nightmare which has all the wealth of exciting action and all the emotional poverty of an adventure story for boys'' to fulfill their yearning for freedom. Here there is a ''state of perpetual emergency and everlasting improvisation.'' The phenomena of an empirically ordinary world are given. All the voluntary movements are possible but ''any sense of direction, any knowledge of where on earth one has come from or where on earth one is going to is completely absent.'' Other selves exist, but no one knows who are his friends or enemies, what is going on, what his own role is. From this ''nightmare of public solitude there is no escape: the inevitable end is ''a serious despair, the love nothing, the fear all.'' The alternative routes, Caliban concludes, the ''facile, gland-handed highway'' or ''the virtuous averted track'' take man to the ''abruptly dreadful end.'' Both are marked by an absence of a commitment. Either way, man is damned since he has tried to avoid the initial choice. Like the artist, he has asked for what he thought he wanted and deserved, and, like him, he thought was choosing Ariel and ended up with Caliban, he has received precisely that which he does not want.

Towards the close of his speech, in a mood of resignation and a hope "that I have had the futile honour of addressing the blind and the deaf," Caliban turns away from the audience to himself. He likens his predicament to "the serio-comic embarrassment of the dedicated dramatist, who, in representing to you your condition of estrangement from the truth, is doomed to fail the more he succeeds." (247) This is the turning point in the character of Caliban as it is the turning point of *The Sea*. Caliban says that the more clearly he sees "the truth," the less able he is to articulate it, and that the closer he comes to articulating "truth," the further he gets from our "condition." Further, even if he is able to articulate both the "truth" and our "condition of estrangement," he must indicate that there is a way to proceed from one to the other even if he is only able to say that "an awareness of the gap is itself a bridge."

Once art confronts man with his true self in order that he moves towards a reconstruction of his being, he envisions that

> Wholly Other Life from which we are separated by an essential emphatic gulf of which our contrived fissures of mirrors and proscenium arch . . . are feebly figurative signs, so that all our meanings are reversed and it is precisely in its negative image of Judgment that we can positively envisage Mercy; it is just here, among the ruins and the bones, that we may rejoice in the perfected work which is not ours. Its great coherences stand out . . . its voice speaks . . . its spaces greet us with all their grand old prospect of wonder and width; the working charm is the full bloom of the unbothered state; the sounded note is the restored relation. (250)

One might find it surprising that Caliban, who in Shakespeare's play symbolizes unregenerated man, should have in Auden's work the last word as it were on art and morality, art and life, man and God and such other profound questions. A close examination of Auden's projection of Caliban would suggest that it couldn't be otherwise if only for the reason that he himself seems an abortive attempt at the realization of the identity of the divine conception of man and God-created world. The deliberate tone of debunking adopted by Caliban in respect of the artist and his powers is suggestive of man's attempts to answer moral questions with physical ones, aesthetic questions with existential ones, not to speak of man's succumbing to the idealistic sense of God's image in man's soul in art if not in life.

Besides "the problem posed by the characters—how one gets off the stage of life, and into what, if anything is real beyond it,"[35] besides Caliban's concern "not with art versus life but with both versus Divine,"[36] *The Sea and the Mirror* "achieves the rare privilege of becoming conscious of itself, and particularly of its reception by ourselves, its audience; so that deprived of a disinterested vantage point outside the poem, and suddenly having become its subject matter, we are placed in the position of having to achieve the reconciliation in our own lives."[37] Thematically it is Kierkegaardian in its emphasis on the value of religious stage of life and technically closer to Brecht since it addresses the audience directly and insists on their participation.

The "Postscript" (ARIEL to CALIBAN. Echo by the PROMPTER) has a lyric sung by Ariel to Caliban about their inseparability and imminent togetherness. Their existences are so tied and intertwined that neither can ignore the other. Imagination may ignore the chaos of life but it does so at the expense of fascinating material. It is not in spite of Caliban but with Caliban that life is complete and true. Human personality comprises Caliban as well as Ariel who make human beings puzzling and fascinating. It has been pointed out that "Auden has subtly and brilliantly exposed the contradictions that govern both art and life" but "has not (despite Caliban's confident and persuasive rationality) been able to show how they may be resolved, except by this gesture towards deity."[38] Ariel's song projects the totality of the individual by placing man at the centre of things.

The Sea and the Mirror, hailed rightly as a masterpiece, has a complex of ideas and styles organized tautly with its components balanced and interwoven with one another. Dealing with the relation of Art and Life in the guise of an art work commenting on another art, the poem achieves a brilliance rarely attained by others. Freud's explanation of art as fantasy and of the artist as a neurotic whose art is a substitute for honour, power, and the love of women, Kierkegaard's emphasis on the religious existence ("a man must get out of the poetical and into the existential"), the inter-dependence of imagination and reality are all so mixed to make the work a mixed perfected brew. The indeterminacy of the structure of *The Sea* is helpful to the presentation of a discussion of vital problems concerning art and artist, himself and his art, apart from his existentialist views, though it leads to a kind of unresolvable aporia.

NOTES

1. The work appeared as a companion piece to *For the Time Being* in 1944. Monroe K Spears citing Auden's letter to him as evidence says that *The Sea and the Mirror* was written after *For the Time Being* between 1942 and 1944. See: *The Poetry of Auden*, pp. 218, 246, 247.
2. Auden, "Criticism in a Mass Society" (1941), quoted in Barbara Everett, p. 77.
3. Charles Osborne, *W.H. Auden: The Life of a Poet* (London: Papermac, 1982), p. 32.
4. W.H. Auden, *The Dyer's Hand and Other Essays* (New York: Faber, 1962), p. 130.
5. *Ibid.*, p. 526.
6. Blair, p. 108.
7. Bahlke, p. 116.
8. Monroe K. Spears, p. 247.
9. Edward Callan, "Auden's Ironic Masquerade: Criticism as Morality Play," *Journal of University of Toronto Quarterly*, 35, 2 (1966), p. 134.
10. *Loc. cit.*
11. *Ibid.*, p. 135.
12. *The Collected Longer Poems* (London: Faber, 1968).
13. Frederick P.W. McDowell, "The Sea and the Mirror," *Auden: A Collection of Critical Essays*, Twentieth Century Views, ed. Monroe K. Spears, p. 143.
14. Spears, p. 220.
15. Blair, p. 109.

16. McDowell, p. 144.
17. Fuller, p. 159.
18. Frederick P.W. McDowell, p. 147.
19. Hoggart, p. 174.
20. W.H. Auden, *The Enchafed Flood* (New York: Vintage Books, Random House, 1967), p. 95.
21. Callan, p. 137.
22. In *The Enchafed Flood* (1950), Auden discusses the sea and the desert symbols very elaborately. See, pp. 5-38.
23. Callan, p. 138.
24. Spears, p. 223.
25. Fuller, pp. 161-62.
26. Bahlke, p. 107.
27. G.S. Fraser, "The Career of Auden," *Auden: A Collection of Critical Essays* ed. M.K. Spears, p. 93.
28. Callan, p. 141.
29. Joseph Warren Beach, *The Making of the Auden Canon* (Minneapolis, 1957), p. 207.
30. Barbara Everett, pp. 78-79.
31. Richard Hoggart, p. 177.
32. Nicholas Rowe, "Solemn and Poetical Magic," *The Tempest*, Casebook Series, ed. D.J. Palmer (London: Macmillan), p. 35.
33. Bahlke, p. 114.
34. Spears, p. 226.
35. Gerald Nelson, *Changes of Heart*, p. 51.
36. Spears, p. 229.
37. Greenberg, p. 123.
38. Fuller, p. 165.

The Age of Anxiety: A Baroque Eclogue

W.H. Auden's *The Age of Anxiety* (1947) is perhaps his most ambitious work if considered in terms of his thematics. It is in this work Auden uses a setting which is both contemporary and eschatological—a setting provided by the Third Avenue Bar during the Second World War. Such a setting affords enough scope for considering such questions as the implications of changing or changed sociological and psychological conditions for contemporary man's philosophy of existence. The "fateful gap between religion and culture" which marks the present condition of man is the focus of Auden's thematic concern besides such other issues suggestive of the failure of faith and the tragic estrangement of man's life, spiritual and otherwise from its own ground and depth which give rise to anxiety in whatever sense it might be considered. The "anxiety" which this work speaks of "embraces not only Freudian 'Angst' but also the Kierkegaardian anxiety which accompanies the paradoxical situation of freedom and of finiteness in which man finds himself, his transcendence of and involvement in nature."[1] Also this work dramatizes through its figures and situations Niebuhr's discussion of the nature of anxiety and his definition of the human condition. For Niebuhr, anxiety is not synonymous with sin:

> Anxiety . . . must be distinguished from sin partly because it is its precondition and not its actuality, and partly because it is the basis of all human creativity as well the precondition of sin. Man is anxious not only because his life is limited and dependent and yet not so limited that he does not know his limitations. He is also anxious because he does not know the

> limits of his possibilities. . . . All human actions stand under seemingly limitless possibilities.[2]

Whether Freudian, Kierkegaardian or Niebuhrian, man's anxiety tends to get aggravated or become all the more pronounced during such cataclysmic events or time of historical acceleration as the Second World War which virtually left man in cultural and spiritual ruins.

Auden presents in this work multiple perspectives on the struggle of the human consciousness to achieve that kind of "pure synthesis" which would ensure a sense of ontological certitude to contemporary man. This does not involve, in so far as Auden is concerned, any conflict between exegesis and dogmatics since his interest is in the exploration of the paradox centering on the finitude of man seeking a dialectical identity in the infinite. In other words, Auden's consideration of the travails of human consciousness is related to the quest of an ontology which confines itself to the structure of finitude embracing the various aspects of modern man's being and its coordinates like freedom and determinism.

Auden subtitles his poem "Baroque Eclogue" which necessitates superimposition of pastoral setting on a contemporary scene. He uses pastoral elements in the poem— "The Dirge," (101-6) a singing contest, (117-22) the courtship of a shepherdess, (55) and the stichomythic dialogue. It is ironical that the pastoral form here presents a world directly opposite the traditional pastoral world. The poem is in a sense a mock-pastoral. The satirical nature of pastoral poetry justifies Auden's use of traditional pastoral elements in this poem. "Baroque" in the title indicates the extravagant quality of the poem, "full of violent contrasts and incongruities, reflecting the stresses of a baroque age."[3] The severely stylized nature of the poem renders it impenetrable and the Anglo-Saxon meter with its four heavy stresses and constant alliteration makes it mock-heroic.

The structure of *The Age of Anxiety* is not new. Auden has traced out portraying the four faculties of the fractured psyche through the four characters in *The Ascent of F6*—Edward Lamp, Ian Shawcross, Gunn and the Doctor, members of the climbing expedition to F6 externally but parts of Michael Ransom's psyche internally. In *For the Time Being,* once again Auden represents the splintered psyche of the fallen man in Intuition, Feeling, Thought and Sensation in the section "The Annunciation." The minor theme of *The Ascent of F6* and *For the Time Being* becomes the major idea in *The Age of Anxiety* since Auden's purpose in it is an investigation of the complex relationship of the four faculties as indicated by Jungian (The process of the Psyche) as incorporated in the thoughts of the characters who are real though representative of the faculties.

The Age of Anxiety has six parts: Parts I and VI form the "Prologue" and "Epilogue," Parts II and III called respectively "The Seven Ages" and "The Seven Stages" are followed by Parts IV and V called "The Dirge" and "The Masque." While Part II echoes Jaques's speech in *As You Like It*, Part III is in the traditional quest pattern.

The "Prologue" begins with a reference to the breaking down of historical process and the preparation for war. It is in wartime that man is "reduced to the anxious status of a shady character or a displaced person" and even the "prudent become worshippers of chance." (255-56). People gather at bars to seek escape in drink and attempt vainly to evade reality. On an All Souls Night, four lonelies Quant, Malin, Rosetta and Emble meet one another by chance at a Third Avenue Bar. Quant, a clerk in a shipping office, is a tired old widower. Professionally, he is a failure although his intelligence is far superior to his position. Malin, a Medical Intelligence Officer in the Canadian Air Force, is the most intelligent and he is to play an important role in the poem. Rosetta, a Jewish department store buyer, is a day-dreamer but her being a Jewess makes her feel insecure and anxious. Finally, there is Emble, a handsome college sophomore, who is anxious about himself and his future. At the level of psychological allegory, Quant represents Intuition, Malin Thinking, Rosetta Feeling and Emble Sensation. In Jungian terms, Thought and Feeling are evaluative functions and Intuition and Sensation are perceptive functions of the psyche. It has been suggested that the four individuals in the poem correspond to Auden's classification of heroes following Kierkegaard in *The*

Enchafed Flood. According to this classification, Emble is a potential aesthetic hero endowed with exceptional gifts but one who is unable to find a quest. Malin is the ethical hero, has superior knowledge but unlike the religious hero he is not absolutely committed. Rosetta and Quant, like Emble, are aesthetic heroes. At the allegorical level, the four characters conform to Jung's classification of psyche. But interestingly enough, they exist in their own right. Their chance encounter is framed by the classical erotic triangle and it may be described as a mystical encounter.

The "Prologue" presents the four characters beginning with Quant and each of them begins by thinking aloud in soliloquies. In his interior monologue, Quant is communing with his mirror image:

> My deuce, my double, my dear image,
> Is it lively there, that land of glass
> Where song is a grimace, sound logic
> A suite of gestures? (258)

He looks at his image and admires it. He is conscious of his intuitive character. Malin is shown thinking about the nature of man:

> Man has no mean; his mirrors distort;
> His greenest arcadias have ghosts too;
> His utopias tempt to eternal youth
> Or self-slaughter. (259)

Rosetta is imaginatively reliving the innocent past obviously disgusted with the present. Emble in relating himself to the others is critical of them. Commenting on the "Prologue," Nelson remarks: "The characters seem to balance one another: Quant's imaginary present with Rosetta's imaginary past—both illusions, both intensely personal—and Malin's comments on man in general with Emble's remarks on the particular people in the bar—both objective, both at least attempting to deal with the immediate world."[5]

While the four individuals live in their isolated worlds, the radio "suddenly breaking in with its banal noises upon their separate senses of themselves . . . began without their knowledge, to draw these four strangers closer to each other." (261) The "official doctored message" narrates the day's incidents. Now the four respond to the description of horror and death, also in interior monologues, and each of the monologues ends with the refrain, "Many have perished: more will." Edward Callan suggests that in this part of the "Prologue," the characters "progress from self-awareness to awareness of a world of objects."[6]

Once the radio ends its broadcast with a commerical, the four open out and begin speaking to each other. They talk about the grisly horrors of the present. Emble in contrast to Rosetta's "Numbers and nightmares have news value" and Malin's "A crime has occurred, accusing all," voices a liberal attitude saying, "Better this than barbarian misrule." Malin says that there is nothing to choose between the old and new worlds, that war is the normal condition.

All that exists
Matters to man; he minds what happens
And feels he is at fault, a fallen soul
With power to place, to explain every
What in his world but why he is neither
God nor good, this guilt the insoluble
Final fact, infusing his private
Nexus of needs, his noted aims with
Incomprehensible comprehensive dread
At not being what he knows that before
This world was he was willed to become. (271-72)

Their conversation on the modern man is interrupted by the radio. The four now come together, form a community, a significant step toward integration. Quant suggests the theme and Rosetta suggests that they move from the bar stools to the quieter intimacy of a booth. As Edward Callan suggests, the "high wooden stools" had been symbols of their isolation, the booth becomes a symbol of what Jung calls "fourness." He quotes Jung in support: "A perception of the significance of fourness, or the totality of the psychic structure, means illumination of the 'inner region.' This recognition is a first step, a necessary station on the road of inner development.''[7]

Part II of *The Age of Anxiety*, "The Seven Ages" is reminiscent of Jaques in *As You Like* It. The newly formed society of four individuals discusses the life of man—from childhood to old age. Malin begins the discussion and speaks on each of the seven ages. Quant, Rosetta and Emble react and respond in their own way drawing on their past, present and hypothetical future. Malin describes in Freudian terms the infant "helpless in cradle and/ Righteous still, yet already there is/Dread in his dreams." (274) He passes on to describe the youth, the second age of man. This is the age when man realizes that "He has laid life-bet with a lying self." (276) Yet man has romantic notions about himself and his boundless energies. He "Pictures as he plods his promised chair/In their small circle secret to those/With no analogies, unique persons,/The originals' ring, the round table/Of master minds." (277) The third age is that of sexual awareness when "alien bodies/Whose figures fasten on his free thoughts." (279) He must shake off his dream images as "he learns what real/Images are." Man realizes that his dreams of love are not true since he encounters the actual presence of another, and while "learning to love, at length he is taught/To know he does not." (279)

The Fourth Age describes man emerging from the dominion of Eros into the real world of "theology and horses." (282) In the Fifth Age, man gains worldly success. Malin presents him as "an astonished victor... at last/Recognition surrounds his days." (284) Having succeeded in making peace with life, "He learns to speak/ Softer and slower, not to seem so eager." (284) His anxiety lessened, he now finds the world a dull, bland place. In the Sixth Age, Malin goes on, man is aging, anxious and unhappy. Man now pines "for some/Nameless Eden where . . . the children play. . . ./ Since they needn't know they're not happy." (288) As Nelson remarks, "Impotent, aged, and successful, Malin's man of the sixth age is past the point of worrying and almost past the point of caring."[8] In the Seventh Age, Malin says, man's "last illusions have lost patience/With the human enterprise. The end comes: he/ Joins the majority, the Jaw-dropped/Mildewed mob and is modest at last." (292)

Quant, Rosetta and Emble respond to Malin's account of the Seven Ages. Malin provides a theoretical understanding, while the comments of the others, which are personal, reveal the nature of their failings. When Malin introduces the first age, the period of childhood, the individual "looks at grown-ups/With conscious care," but, despite this, existence is mainly immediate, tied to the "Instant Present." Because of the strong influence of imagination on the shadowy inner life of "Feelings through facts," this is the period of solipsism, for Quant a time when tires could be "burned alive," for Emble when he could bring punishment from heaven upon tormenting cousins, for Rosetta when her "dearest doll was deaf and spoke in/Grunts like grandfather." As Greenberg observes, "Convincingly typical as they are, there is a glimpse of the older person in each of these reminiscences. In Quant's case, it is simply that the grimy unpromising environment of childhood foreshadows the beaten man, but Emble's delusion of exceptional powers and Rosetta's belief in secret arrangements already indicate the devices they will use to keep from self-acceptance."[9]

To Malin's account of the second age, of adolescence, the normal beginning of the journey of life, a time of self-pity and of the fantasies, Quant remembers his adolescence when he imagined himself a rich tycoon with sirens at his disposal; Emble, "After a dreadful/Row with father," consoles himself that "fifty years hence/Massed choirs would sing as my coffin passed,/Grieved for and great on a gun-carriage;" Rosetta's adolescence is filled with fancies of "The house on the headland I would own one day."

To Malin's description of the Third Age, the age of young manhood, Rosetta and Emble speak of disillusionment in love. Quant tells the "long/Visitors' voyage to Venus Island" and can't see difference between love and lust. In the Fourth Age, man "finds out/Where his world lies." Rosetta in her regression protests, "Too soon we embrace that/Impermanent appetitive flux... which adults fear/Is real and right." Emble remarks that this "real" world is full of perversions of Eros. In the Fifth Age, according to Malin, man's life is marked by success. Emble's speech shows that he is the only character bound by youth, that he suffers "from that anxiety about himself and his future which haunts, like a bad smell, the minds of most young men." He is annoyed by time in a way different from Quant or Rosetta, for he is still young enough to demand a future from the world—he wants an answer from the world. Quant warns Emble that he "will no longer/Expect more pattern, more purpose than/Your finite fate." He predicts for Emble defeatist submission and declares his belief in the futility of existence. When Emble and Rosetta demand purpose and results in man's life, Quant says that future is "Nowhere." There is no future because men live in the present where hope can never be realized. Life goes nowhere because there is nowhere for it to go. Quant dominates this part and hence the fifth age is the most depressing. All hope is eliminated. Man has to adjust to mediocrity and cannot ask for more. In the Sixth Age, man "takes pills for vigour/And sound sleep, and sees in his mirror/The jawing genius of a jackass age,/A rich bore." (288) The old age is accompanied by dissatisfaction and discontent. The individual regrets his past and yearns "for some/Nameless Eden where he never was." Quant admits that he has entertained such a wish recounting his quest for the fairy-tale treasure and concedes his consciousness of guilt. Rosetta and Emble join in the lament, he for the "garden," she for the innocence of a play-thing world. When Malin passes on to the Seventh Age, the three return to their illusions. Rosetta returns to her Innocent Landscape. Emble compares himself with the Average. Quant seeks refuge in humour and cynicism.

The philosophic discussion of "The Seven Ages" fails to offer a solution to the problems encountered by the participants. Therefore, Quant intuitively chooses Rosetta to lead them on their quest: "O show us the route/Into hope and health; give each the required/ Pass to appear the superior archons;/Be our good guide." (295) Rosetta wonders what gift of direction is entrusted to her to lead them on the journey homeward "through the Maze of Time,/ Seeking its centre," but agrees to seek the "Regressive road to Grandmother's house." Since Malin's guided tour did not lead them to happiness, they are contemplating a journey in the other direction, towards "that state of pre-historic happiness" "The Quiet Kingdom."

Part II ends with the narrator's brief speech which suggests that in a state of semi-intoxication, members of a group "establish a rapport in which communication of thoughts and feelings is so accurate and instantaneous, that they appear to function as a single organism." (296) The narrator says that Rosetta commences a journey leading them all into the unconscious where their psychic differences submerge: "The more completely these four forgot their surroundings and lost their sense of time, the more sensitively aware of each other they became, until they achieved in their dream that rare community which is otherwise only attained in states of extreme wakefulness. But this did not happen all at once." (296)

Part III, "The Seven Stages," based on the Quest Pattern, is a parody-quest for an un-recoverable Innocence. The journey through "The Seven Ages" is a realistic one in that a group of people sit and discuss their experiences, whereas the journey through "The Seven Stages" is non-realistic. Together, Parts II and III, Bahlke suggests, form a "Dream Quest": "The seven divisions in each part correspond in a generalized way to the seven circles of Dante's Purgatorio."[10] There is a closer link between Dante's seven cycles of Purgation and Kierkegaard's concept of Anxiety as the springboard for the leap of faith.

In this first stage of the journey each of the four "walks alone" in "dark," sharing a "feeling of remoteness and desertion" with lost bearings and restless urge to find water. They pass through a mountainous district where each has a vision of mankind's struggle into consciousness in which images of peaks, hills, banks and mountains recur. Frightened of being alone, they move from "the high heartland to the maritime plains" coupling "youth with youth and age with age." This grouping begins the second stage of the journey which ends for Rosetta and Emble that there is escape from self through the romance of youth and for Quant and Malin through the resignation to age. In the third stage of their journey, they turn to inland again towards a common goal the city, Emble and Rosetta by plane, Malin and Quant by train. In the fourth stage, there is a discussion of the city, "a facetious culture" which outwardly is well-planned and orderly. From the city, they go to "the big house" by a trolley car. Rosetta, who always dreams of a mansion, exclaims: "In I shall go, out I shall look." For Quant "The facade has a lifeless look." For Rosetta, it means isolation and selfishness of created things:

> I have watched through a window a world that is fallen,
> The mating and malice of men and beasts,
> The corporate greed of quiet vegetation,
> And the homesick little obstinate sobs of things thrown into being. (314)

The sixth stage brings them to the hermetic gardens whose extraordinary charm begins to work upon them and they all become uneasy and unwell. The charm of the gardens seems to the characters to be an accusation, a ridicule of their impotence. Quant is uneasy and dissatisfied with what he has, Emble with his Don Juanism, Rosetta with her snobbery and Malin with his intellectual narcissism.

Loaded with guilt and obsessed by imaginary ills, the four "plunge into the labyrinthine forest and vanish down solitary paths, with no guide but their sorrows, no companion but their own voices." (322) They wander through the forest in despair and finally meet at the forest's edge. Here they become aware of their own defects or forms of pride. They are led to the Desert, the place of trial, where their doubts assail them. Malin says: "It takes will to cross this waste/Which is really empty." Then he asks the central question, an important one in the context of the entire poem: "Do I love this world so well/That I have to know how it ends?" (325) While they stand caught by this question and the fear that there really is no meaning, no positive solution to the problem of existence, the desert turns into the real world "from which their journey has been one long flight." At the end of their mock quest, the four at the suggestion of Rosetta go to her apartment.

As Malin, Quant, Emble and Rosetta go in a cab to Rosetta's apartment, they compose a lament which forms Part IV of *The Age of Anxiety*, "The Dirge." Fuller suggests that "The Dirge" "appears to be an elegy for Franklin D. Roosevelt concerted into a generalized lament for the passing of secular law givers who are the heroes of the City,"[11] "some semi-divine stranger with superhuman powers, some Gilgamesh or Napoleon, some Solon or Sherlock Holmes (who) appeared from time to time to rescue both man and nature, for a brief bright instant, from their egregious destructive blunders." (330) The lament is for the absence of a "saviour" in the present day. The four, instead of searching within themselves for the answers to the problems they confront, bemoan the absence of a leader. Their leader, hero, saviour, is one who will assume the responsibility for their inadequacies but not one who will demand an equal responsibility from them.

Part V of *The Age of Anxiety* called "The Masque" climaxes the action of the work. At Rosetta's apartment, "all felt that it was time something exciting happened and decided to do their best to see that it did." Rosetta and Emble, attracted to each other sexually, dance to Quant's and Malin's songs and sing together. In the course of their singing and dancing, amidst the prayers and benedictions of Quant and Malin, Rosetta's and Emble's mutual attraction becomes more obvious "and of immense importance." The lovers and the separators recognize this and they all begin a masque which is "both a mock marriage mass and a fertility rite."[12] Malin, like the priest, offers an invocation to Venus and it is followed by exchange of vows by Emble and Rosetta. After seeing off Malin and Quant, Rosetta returns to her apartment to find Emble asleep in her bedroom and "passed out." In a long soliloquy, she expresses her recognition that as a jewess she can never realize any permanent meaningful relationship between herself and Emble. She thinks of the differences in background that would make their love a casual one. Her Jewish heritage and racial differences would be a great obstacle to her love. She knows that there is no peace for her, no escape from her guilt until she is able to face herself as she is and her past as it was: "I shan't be at peace/Till I really take your restless hands,/My poor fat father." (347) She concludes with a confession of faith in Hebrew: the Shema which proclaims the unity of God.

Part VI, "The Epilogue" with which the poem concludes, consists of Quant's "improptu ballad" sung as he walks home, and

Malin's musings as he rides the subway home. Quant's song ridicules "The Victory Powers" as they foolishly destroy the defeated. Malin's thoughts center round the foolishness of the characters's quest:

> Age softens the sense of defeat
> As well as the will to success,
> Till the unchangeable losses of childhood.
> The forbidden affections rebel
> No more; so now in the mornings
> I wake, neither warned nor refreshed,
> From dreams without daring, a series
> Of vaguely disquieting adventures
> Which never end in horror,
> Brief or forgiving embraces. (348)

Malin says that man doesn't learn from the past, that the future is bleak. Man cannot understand the relation between time and eternity, the "clock we are bound to obey/And the miracle we must not despair of"; he cannot imagine Agape the "raging lion is to time/With the yearning Unicorn." (351) Neither reason nor imagination can enable us to comprehend realities. There is a need for change but man avoids it: "We would rather die in our dread/Than climb the cross of the moment/And let our illusions die." (350) The choice is not easy because it is "too obvious and near to notice" and is "reserved/For the eyes of faith to find," (351) and our own efforts, without grace, cannot achieve faith.

Edward Callan finds two kinds of allegory in *The Age of Anxiety*, one psychological and the other spiritual, the machinery of which derives from the psychological theories of Jung and from the existentialist philosophies of Heidegger, Jaspers and Kierkegaard as well as from the mainstream of Judeo-Christian belief. Jung's concept of the disintegration of the psyche is represented by Malin (Thought), Rosetta (Feeling), Quant (Intuition), and Emble (Sensation), who explores the allegorical landscape, the landscape of psyche encompassing the realms of personal and collective unconscious. At the level of spiritual allegory, the characters represent the disintegrated faculties inherited from the Fall. After discussing the structure of each of the six parts of *The Age,* he says that some familiarity with Jung's theories is valuable for a full understanding of the work: "Indeed, it might reasonably be said that Jung's work, particularly *Modern Man in Search of a Soul*, is related to *The Age of Anxiety* much as Jessie Weston's *From Ritual to Romance* is to *The Waste Land.*"[13]

Barbara Everett's reading of the poem's form, its use of the device of contrast and comparison, is interesting. She says that the form of *The Age* places the characters in a "contradictory context which at one and the same time stresses their distance from the Innocent, yet suggests that, as the eclogue form itself shows Innocence only through sophisticated Artifice, so may these characters at any moment cross, if they will, into the Garden, the Good Place, the World of Innocence.... A way is opened out of the crowd into a pastoral community: but they refuse to take it." The second device of contrast and comparison is that the characters are continually placed against "Langland's *Piers Plowman*, the magnificent account of a search for Christ that begins in a Field of Folk, moves outward to the Crucifixion and the Harrowing of Hell, and returns at the end to the confused and troubled world with which it began."[14]

Though *The Age of Anxiety* is full of minute brilliances, and packed with fascinating definitions, descriptions, epigrams, the commentators point to the absence of the large organizing design, call it too artificial and rhetorical, lacking in dramatic quality, and as a war poem or a tract of the times, unrealistic and superficial. Randall Jarrell was very unsympathetic to *The Age*, when he wrote:

> *The Age of Anxiety* is the worst thing Auden has written since "The Dance of Death"; it is the equivalent of Wordsworth's "Ecclesiastical Sonnets." The man, who, during the thirties, was one of the five or six best poets in the world has gradually turned into a rhetoric mill grinding away at the bottom of Limbo, into an automaton that keeps making little jokes, little plays on words, little rhetorical engines, as compulsively and unendingly and uneasily as a neurotic washes his hands.[15]

Criticism of this kind is largely coloured by prejudice against Auden's migration and subsequent religious conversion rather than sympathy. Spears cites the opposite instance of Leonard Bernstein who was inspired by the poem and who called it "fascinating and hair-raising."

John Bayley eulogizes *The Age of Anxiety* as Auden's greatest achievement to date, and the one which best shows the true nature of his scope and talent."[16] He warms upto the modesty and sympathy of tone, the effects of tenderness and pathos and links Auden both to the Romantics and to the novel. Spears admires Bayley's perceptive criticism but wonders what kind of coherence and unity the "exuberance of particularity" or the "trivia of the consciousness" form to make *The Age* a good poem. Provocative and fascinating ideas apart, it is uneven: "It is not as rich nor varied nor profound as either *For the Time Being* or *The Sea and the Mirror*. . . . But it is a brilliant and moving and impressive performance, and one we would not willingly be without."[17]

Herbert Greenberg, though not inclined to question the general judgment concerning an overall lack of dramatic conflict in *The Age*, nevertheless admires it for "much accomplished verse and a good deal of genuine if somewhat abstract insight into human living: it is difficult to evaluate justly because many of its effects do not simply fail—they alienate."[18] Edward Callan lays stress on Auden's tendency to seize upon the artistic or "shaping" possibilities that a particular theory or ideas of thinkers may provide for the poetic imagination. He concludes his discussion of *The Age* with the following account: "*The Age of Anxiety* is an ambitious and ingenious work of art, even though it gives the impression, in places, of having been 'roughed out' rather than carefully polished. . . . But it is a significant work pioneering imaginatively in unfamiliar territory; and it was well described by Marianne Moore as "a deep and fearless piece of work matched by a mechanics of consummate virtuosity."[19]

In conclusion, it might be said that Auden's *The Age of Anxiety* is distinguished not only by its subject matter which is of profound concern to the contemporary world but also by its unique blend of styles. Its sub-title draws pointed attention to what is characteristic of the cultural history of man which is exemplified by "an oscillation between a predominantly rational world view and alternate spasms of irrational and subjective endeavours" as exemplified by the baroque. This highlights Auden's preoccupation with the question of the evolving consciousness—asesthetic, psychological and historical—under the pressure of history which accounts for the "new evolutionary hopes and desires and new underlying forces, psychic and social." It is not surprising that the characters in this dramatic work function not only symbolically as different aspects of consciousness but also as registers of consciousness which seem capable of engendering new concepts of mental and emotional dissociation which spells the tragicality of man's situation in this world.

NOTES

1. Bahlke, p. 133.
2. *Loc. cit.*
3. Monroe K. Spears, p. 231.
4. W.H. Auden, *The Age of Anxiety: A Baroque Eclogue in Collected Longer Poems* (London: Faber, 1968).
5. Gerald Nelson, *Changes of Heart: A Study of the Poetry of W.H. Auden* (Berkeley: University of California Press, 1969), p. 82.
6. Edward Callan, "Allegory in Auden's '*The Age of Anxiety*,'" *Twentieth-Century Literature*, 10, 4 (1965), p. 158.
7. *Loc. cit.*
8. Nelson, p. 89.
9. Greenberg, p. 159.
10. Bahlke, p. 137.
11. Fuller, p. 198.
12. Nelson, p. 100.
13. Callan, p. 163.
14. Barbara Everett, pp. 87-88.
15. Randall Jarrell, quoted in Spears's *The Poetry of Auden*, p. 239.

16. John Bayley, *The Romantic Survival: A Study in Poetic Revolution* (London: Constable, 1957), p. 185.
17. Spears, pp. 240-41.
18. Greenberg, p. 168.
19. Callan, p. 164.

Conclusion

There are no two opinions about Auden being one of the most significant poets of the present century. An acknowledged metrical genius, prolific and purposeful from the beginning, Auden "the sage of anxiety" offers more than any single poet the image of the times, its pressures, its distortions, its high and low points. We would be doing less than justice to Auden's mastery of the word and his wide-ranging meaning, its profundity and depth if we mistake what is often referred to as his lightness of touch for anything other than deep, serious and even tragic on occasion. Much of the importance of his work to English poetry is traceable to its providing a literary record of "the disintegrating collision in a sensitive mind of the old tradition and new learning" as T.S. Eliot's does. Hailed as a liberating influence, Auden has unceasingly experimented with a variety of forms of poetry which has had the effect of animating them with a new vitality and what is more a new relevance to modern conditions. A close examination of his poetry would reveal that he has restored to English poetry its dramatic sense and a kind of complexity realized through the playing of fantasy against realism, silence against sound, and the existential against the experiential. His use of cinematographic techniques in the structuring of his poetry has enlarged the scope of imagism in poetry in such a way as to invest it with the power of the "moving image." Interestingly, his quest for fresh poetic utterances has not resulted in his rejection of formal verse systems as it seems to have in the works of his contemporaries. Indeed, his choice of form has at all times been dictated by its flexibility and range demanded by the envisaged poem. Integral to it is his metaphor predicated on live myths which enables him to dissolve the pattern of abstract experience into a living image of man or human reality. Again the complex of styles which mark his poetic idiom points to his interest in the distillation of language that can possibly articulate the rhythms of living experience.

As has been pointed out by several literary historians, the tone of most English poets of the forties and fifties in respect of both technique and attitude was derived from Auden's poetry which should not surprise any discriminating reader. Auden seems to have provided to his younger contemporaries a model for a structure of the poet's encounter with the world and with his art derived from the dominant structures of thought of his time, structures or systems like the Marxist, the Freudian and the existentialist. A striking example is that of Philip Larkin who can be said to have found himself only when he has been able to invest his poetry with such a kind of "social annotations and self-deprecating tone" as has come to characterize Auden's poetry. This is not to suggest that Larkin has no "voice" of his own or that he handles the consciously held idea in the way that Auden does. But it is that he seems as intent as Auden in realizing such a kind of relationship between his art and the society in which and for which he explores the potentialities innate to the exercise of his creative power. This explains why his poetry could be regarded as "a clearing house for modern psychology and social doctrine," not to speak of the new aesthetic concepts and ideas. The topicality of his poetry is illustrative of the new equation sought to be realized between the poet and the world through a direct confrontation even if it were to result in poet's revenge upon the world.

Auden's plays essentially indistinguishable from his longer poems represent a memorable experiment with dramaturgy and dramatic irony suggestive of a breakthrough on the part of English drama to a freer force demanded by the modernist sensibility. The mythologizing of social issues raised by or figuring in his plays is of a piece with his secularization of spiritual concerns and the apprehension of the immediacy and the urgency of what is historically local through the planes and conjunctions accessible to the fictionalizing mind. But Auden might at all times be found structuring or ordering his work out in terms of the sequence of historical time or evolution of character on an evolving pattern of images reflecting states of consciousness and sticking to the logic of metaphor.

The Auden-Isherwood joint authorship, one of the happiest and the most creative of collaborations in literary history, affords the lesson that creative enterprise need not necessarily be a solo performance. Traditionally the theatre brings together the producer, the playwright, the actor, the costume maker, the singer expecting them to work harmoniously for the success of the play's production. Drama, unlike the other species of writing, has thus been a collaborative act whose performance is dictated by total involvement of a variety of talents. The Auden-Isherwood collaboration is distinctive in that it draws the poet in Auden and the novelist in Isherwood closer so that their plays combine poetic precision and prose discourse to the best advantage. The process of collaboration of the Auden-Isherwood kind subjecting the text to alterations and revisions, is itself a fascinating study as has been shown in the reading of the plays. For example, there are as many as three drafts for *The Dog Beneath the Skin* and there is more than one ending for the plays written in collaboration. It may be noted that Auden's collaboration is not confined to the stage plays he wrote with Isherwood but extends to collaborations on liberators, travel dairies, translations and adaptations. That Auden collaborated not with one but with many, that the forms varied from stage plays to other kinds is significant if only for the reason that it speaks eloquently of Auden's geniality and catholicity.

The importance of Auden's aesthetic ideas for a total theatre has been shown to be considerable comparable to Gordon Craig's and Granville Barker's. As the founder of the Group Theatre, an avant garde experiment, Auden spelt out his theories of drama and its production in the Group Theatre papers. Although the poetics appeared to be original and novel, it cannot be asserted that they signal a break with the conventional and historical. Auden does make use of traditional genres in an attempt to revive and invest them with new life. The naturalistic and the expressionistic mix to project a new type of play. Dream sequences and scenes of symbolic import with no clear time and place follow each other quickly. The surrealist abruptness characterizing *Paid on Both Sides, The Ascent of F6* and *On the Frontier* might result in the seeming looseness of structure but their freedom from the unities render them ideal for psychological probing and for dramatizing moral abstractions. The success of *The Dog Beneath the Skin*, on the other hand, proves the efficacy of Auden's belief that avant garde play should borrow from the techniques of musical comedy or pre-medieval folk play. In a loosely connected series of tableaux, this play dramatizes the rake's progress through a dying culture, the stations of the cross of the death wish followed by the moralizing of the chorus.

The juxtaposition of the ancient and the modern, a method consistently adopted in the plays and the longer poems, is achieved at the level of myth but not at the linguistic. In *Paid on Both Sides* and *The Ascent of F6*, the Aeschylean moral grandeur and the benality of modern attitudes co-exist as they represent as much the umbilical attachment as the feuding communities. The lovers in *On the Frontier*, ill-fated and star-crossed, do not rise to the tragic heights of Tristan and Isolde but approximate to Romeo and Juliet in their pathos. The use of modern idiom, even when the theme is historical or ancient as in *For the Time Being*, makes a work relevant to modern times. The narrator, for example, in *For the Time Being*, is modern while the characters of Herod, Simeon, Joseph, Mary, though ancient, speak in modern idiom. The linguistic approximation breaks the barriers of distance resulting in the increased response of the reader and at the same time preventing any attempt at identification. The Shakespearean characters in *The Sea and the Mirror* speak in different forms which suggest their degrees of transformation and reconciliation. Caliban's dazzling involuted style spoken in the later James manner is suggestive of the complexity of Caliban and Ariel relationship. It might therefore be said that Auden's plays for the theatre achieve a fusion of the parabolic and the didactic and his longer poems compare and contrast the old and new.

The final impression that Auden's work leaves is "Life remains a blessing although we cannot bless." In the early poetry, the psychological doctrine of repression and teleological death wish with its stress on sickness made one feel that life is not worth living. It only made one self-consious and guilty. Marx the political revolutionary by pointing out social corruption contributed to the declining morale of the middle classes. It was left to Auden to find hope in Marx's empirical philosophy, and to show that life remains a blessing. It might be asserted that this belief is central to Auden's work as a whole. Auden goes so far as to support a philosophy that accepted life with all the imperfections. That men are "articled to error" and "never will be perfect like the fountains" suggest their incurable imperfection. The reformist zeal urging men to celebrate their instincts and to overthrow capitalist hegemony noticeable in Auden's early poetry disappears while the emphasis on accepting life begins to appear in every poem after his discovery of Kierkegaard. Kierkegaard provided Auden with not only the philosophical basis for accepting life but theological imperative that it must be accepted. The long poems of the 1940's from *New Year Letter* to *The Age of Anxiety* written in the Christian tradition emphasize that man accept life and not transcend it. The secular existence is to be accepted as part of God's design. Auden's career stretching over four decades appears to be one long struggle to discover the basic affirmations of life in the face of almost sinful indulgence in negation which informs the writings of a majority of writers in this post-modern period.

Indeed, Auden seems assured of his place in the history of modern English poetry probably for his generative sense of style and "complexity of aesthetic enquiry." Civilized, witty and endlessly inventive, a graceful poet full of wisdom and knowledge, "Auden was," in the words of Cyril Connolly, "for many of us the last poet we learnt by heart."

Bibliography

Primary Sources

Poems. Oxford, 1928.
Poems. London: Faber, 1930.
The Orators. London: Faber, 1932.
The Dance of Death. London: Faber, 1933.
Poems. New York: Random House, 1934.
The Dog Beneath the Skin (with Christopher Isherwood). London: Faber, 1935; Random House, 1935.
The Ascent of F6 (with Christopher Isherwood). London: Faber, 1936.
Look Stranger. London: Faber, 1936; as *On this Island*, New York Random House, 1937.
Letters From Iceland (with Louis MacNeice). London: Faber, 1937; New York: Random House, 1937.
On the Frontier (with Christopher Isherwood). London: Faber, 1938; New York: Random House, 1938.
Journey to A War (with Christopher Isherwood). London: Faber, 1939; New York: Random House, 1939.
Another Time. New York: Random House, 1940; London: Faber, 1940.
Some Poems. London: Faber, 1940.
The Double Man. New York: Random House, 1941; as *New Year Letter*, London: Faber, 1941.
For the Time Being. New York: Random House, 1944; London: Faber, 1945.
The Collected Poetry of W.H. Auden. New York: Random House, 1945.
The Age of Anxiety. New York: Random House, 1947; London: Faber, 1948.
The Collected Shorter Poems, 1930-1944. London: Faber, 1950.
The Enchafed Flood. New York: Random House, 1950; London: Faber, 1951.
Nones. New York: Random House, 1951; London: Faber, 1952.
The Rake's Progress (with Chester Kallman). London: Boosey and Hawkes, 1951.
The Shield of Achilles. New York: Random House, 1955; London: Faber, 1955.
W.H. Auden: A Selection by the Author. Penguin, 1958; as *The Selected Poetry of W.H.Auden*, Modern Library, 1959.
Homage to Clio. New York: Random House, 1960; London: Faber, 1960.

Elegy for Young Lovers (with Chester Kallman). Mainz: Schott, 1961.
The Dyer's Hand. New York: Random House, 1962; London: Faber, 1963.
Selected Essays. London: Faber, 1964.
About the House. New York: Random House, 1965; London: Faber, 1966.
The Bassarids (with Chester Kallman). Mainz: Schott, 1966.
Collected Shorter Poems, 1927-1957. London: Faber, 1966; New York: Random House, 1967.
Selected Poems. London: Faber, 1968.
Collected Longer Poems. London: Faber, 1968; New York: Random House, 1969.
Secondary Worlds. London: Faber, 1968; New York: Random House, 1969.
City Without Walls. London: Faber, 1969; New York: Random House, 1970.
A Certain World; a commonplace book. New York: Viking Press, 1970.
Epistle to Godson. New York: Random House, 1972.
Forewords and Afterwords. New York: Random House, 1973.
Thank You, Fog. New York: Random House, 1974.
Collected Poems. Ed. Edward Mendelson. London: Faber, 1976.
The English Auden. Ed. Edward Mendelson. London: Faber, 1977.

Secondary Sources

Allen, Walter. "W.H. Auden: The Most Exciting Living Poet." *Listener*, 47 (17 April 1952), pp. 640-41.
Allot, Kenneth. "Auden in the Theatre." *New Verse*, Nos. 26-27 (November 1937), pp. 17-21.
Alvarez, A. *The Shaping Spirit: Studies in Modern English and American Poets*. London: Chatto and Windus, 1958.
Anderson, D.M. "Aspects of Auden," *Landfall*, 3 (September 1949), pp. 270-79.
Anon. "Sixteen Comments on Auden," *New Verse*, Nos. 26-27 (November 1937), pp. 23-30.
------. "W.H. Auden," *Wilson Bulletin*, 12 (January 1938), p. 362.
Appel, Benjamin, "The Exiled Writers," *Saturday Review of Literature*, 22 (19 October 1940), pp. 3-5.
Bahlke, George W. *The Later Auden:* From *"New Year Letter" to "About the House," Literature in Perspective*. New Brunswick, New Jersey: Rutgers University Press, 1970.
Bailey, Ruth. *A Dialogue on Modern Poetry*. London: Humphrey Milford, Oxford University Press, 1939.
Barker, George. "Review of Books: Collected Shorter Poems, W.H. Auden." *Life and Letters*, 65 (April-June, 1950), pp. 68-70.
Barness, T.R. "Auden and Isherwood." *Scrutiny*, 7 (December 1938), pp. 361-63.

Barzum, Jacques. "Auden on Romanticism," *Yale Review*, 39 (June 1950), pp 730-33.

Bateson, F.W. "Auden's Last Poems." *Essays in Criticism*, 25 (July 1975), pp 383-90.

Bayley, John. "W.H. Auden," *The Romantic Survival; A Study in Poetic Evolution*. London: Constable, 1957, pp. 127-85.

Beach, Joseph Warren. "The Poems of Auden and Prose Diathesis." *Virginia Quarterly Review*, 25 (July 1949), pp. 365-83.

------. *The Making of the Auden Canon*. Minneapolis: University of Minnesota Press, 1957.

------. *Obsessive Images*. Minneapolis: University of Minnesota Press, 1960, pp. 104-13.

Benner Dica. "Wystan Hugh Auden," *Poets of Our Time*. New York: Harcourt, Brace, 1941, pp. 245-77.

Bergonzi, Bernard. *Reading the Thirties: Texts and Pretexts*. University of Pittsburgh Press, 1978.

Blackburn, Thomas. "W.H. Auden," *The Price of an Eye*. London: Longmans, pp. 85-98.

Blair, John G. *The Poetic Art of W.H. Auden*. Princeton: Princeton University Press, 1965.

------. "W.H. Auden: The Poem as Performance." *Shenandoah*, 16 (Spring 1965), pp. 55-66.

Bloom, Robert. "W.H. Auden's Bestiary of the Human." *Virginia Quarterly Review*, 42 (Spring 1966), pp. 207-33.

------. "The Humanization of Auden's Early Style." *PMLA*., 83 (May 1968), pp. 443-54.

Bloomfield, B.C. *W.H. Auden: A Bibliography: The Early Years Through 1955*. Charlottesville: University Press of Virginia, 1964.

Bloomfield, B.C. and Edward Mendelson. *W.H. Auden, A Bibliography*, 1924-1969. Second Ed. Charlottesville, Virginia: University Press of Virginia, 1972.

Braybrooks, Neville. "W.H. Auden: The Road from Marx," *America*, 88 (21 March), pp. 680-81.

Broke-Rose, Christine. "Notes on the Metre of Auden's 'The Age of Anxiety'." *Essays in Criticism*, 13 (July 1963), pp. 253-64.

Brooks, Benjamin Gilbert. "The Poetry of Auden," *Nineteenth Century and After*, 141 (January 1947), pp. 30-40.

Brooks, Cleanth. *Modern Poetry and the Tradition*. Chapel Hill: University of North Carolina Press, 1939, pp. 125-35.

------. "A Descriptive Chart of the Disenchanted Island." *Sewanee Review*, 72 (April-June 1964), pp. 300-6.

------. "W.H. Auden as a Critic." *Kenyon Review*, 26 (Winter 1964), pp. 173-89.

Bruehl, William J. "Polus Naufrangia: A Key Symbol in *The Ascent of F6*."

Modern Drama, 10 (September 1967), pp. 161-64.
Bullough, Geoffrey. "Metaphysicals and Left-Wingers," *The Trend of Modern Poetry*. Edinburgh: Oliver and Boyd, 1934, pp. 160-62.
Buell, Frederick. *W.H. Auden as a Social Poet*. New York: Cornell University Press, 1973.
Burgam, Edwin Berry. "Three English Radical Poets." *New Masses*, 12 (3 July 1934), pp. 33-36.
Burnham, James. "W.H. Auden." *Nation*, 139 (8 August, 1934), pp. 164-65.
Callan, Edward. "The Development of W.H. Auden's Poetic Theory since 1940." *Twentieth-Century Literature*, 4 (October 1954), pp. 79-91.
------. "An Annotated Checklist of the Works of W.H. Auden (1924-1957)." *Twentieth-Century Literature*, 4 (April-July 1958), pp. 30-50.
------. "Auden's *New Year Letter:* A New Style of Architecture." *Renascence*, 16 (Fall 1963), pp. 13-19.
------. "Allegory in Auden's *The Age of Anxiety*." *Twentieth-Century Literature*, 10 (January 1965), pp. 155-65.
------. "Auden and Kierkegaard: The Artistic Framework of *For the Time Being*." *The Christian Scholar*, 48 (Fall 1965), pp.211-23.
------. "Auden's Ironic Masquerade: Criticism as Morality Play." *University of Toronto Quarterly*, 35 (January 1966), pp. 133-43.
------. "Auden's Goodly Heritage." *Shenandoah*, 18 (Winter 1967), pp. 56-68.
------. "W.H. Auden: The Framing of a Verse." *Southern Review*, 2 (April 1967), pp. 341-56.
------. "W.H. Auden: Annotated Checklist II (1958-1969)." *Twentieth-Century Literature*, 16 (January 1970), pp. 27-56.
------. "Auden Triumphant." *Journal of Modern Literature*, 3 (April 1974), pp. 1055-62.
------. W.H. Auden's Plays for the Group Theatre: from revelation to revelation." *Comparative Drama*, 12 (1978), pp. 326-39.
Chase, Richard Volney. *Quest for Myth*. Baton Rouge: Louisiana State University Press, 1949, pp. 127-31.
Clanoy, Joseph. "Auden Waiting for his City." *Christian Scholar*, 42 (Fall 1959), pp. 185-200
Close, H.M. "The Development of Auden's Poetry." *Cambridge Review*, 58 (9 June), pp. 478-79.
Coghill, Nevill. *T.S. Eliot: A Symposium*. Ed. Richard March and Tambimuttu. London: Poetry London, 1948.
Connolly, Cyril. "Remembering Auden." *Encounter*, 44 (March 1975), pp. 90-93.
Cook, F.W. "Primordial Auden." *Essays of Criticism*, 12 (October 1962), pp. 402-12.
Cowley, Malcolm. "Auden in America." *New Republic*, 104 (7 April 1941), pp. 473-74.
"Virtue and Virtuosity: Notes on W.H. Auden." *Poetry*, 65 (January

1945), pp. 202-9.
Cox, R.G. "Auden as Critic and Poet." *Scrutiny*, 18 (Autumn 1951), pp. 158-61.
------. *The Pelican Guide to English Literature*. Vol. 7. Ed. Boris Ford. Harmondsworth: Penguin, 1961, pp. 373-93.
Daalder, Joost. "Yeats and Auden: Some Verbal Parallels." *Notes and Queries*, 20 (September 1973), pp. 334-35.
Daiches, David. "W.H. Auden: The Search for a Public." *Poetry*, 54 (1939), pp. 148-56.
------. "Into the World," *Poetry*, 56 (April 1940), pp. 40-43.
Darlington, W.A. "A Theorist in the Theatre." *Discovery*, 16 (December 1935), pp. 349-51.
Davie, Donald. *Thomas Hardy and British Poetry*. New York: Oxford University Press, 1971.
Davison, Dennis. *W.H. Auden*. Literature in Perspective. London: Evans Brothers, 1970.
Davison, Trevor. "The Method of Auden's 'The Orators.'" *Durham University Journal*, 32 (June 1971), pp. 167-78.
Day Lewis, C. *A Hope for Poetry*. Oxford: Blackwell, 1934.
Dobree, Bonamy. "W.H. Auden." *Shenandoah*, 18 (Winter 1967), pp. 18-22.
Donoghue, Charles. "Auden on Romanticism." *Thought*, 26 (Summer 1951), pp. 283-87.
Donoghue, Denis. *The Third Voice*. Princeton: Princeton University Press, 1959.
Doone, Rupert. "The Theatre of Ideas." *Theatre Newsletter*, 6 (29 September 1951), p. 5.
Drummond, John. "The Mind of Mr. W.H. Auden." *Townsman*, 1, (July 1937), pp. 233-36.
Duchene, Francois. *The Case of the Helmeted Airman; A Study of W.H. Auden's Poetry*. London: Chatto and Windus, 1971.
Dupee, F.W. "W.H. Auden." *The Nation*, 159 (28 October 1944), pp. 537-38.
Ellmann, Richard. *Eminent Domain: Yeats Among Wilde, Joyce, Pound, Eliot and Auden*. New York: Oxford University Press, 1967.
Elton, William. "Metapoetry by a Thinking Type." *Poetry*, 71 (November 1947), pp. 90-94.
Empson, William. "A Note on Auden's 'Paid on Both Sides'." *Experiment*, 7 (Spring 1931), pp. 60-61.
------. "Early Auden." *Review* (Oxford), 5 (February 1963), pp. 32-34.
Engle, Paul. "New English Poets." *English Journal*, 27 (February 1938), pp. 89-101.
Enright, D.J. "Reluctant Admiration: A Note on Auden and Rilke." *Essays in Criticism*, 2 (April 1952), pp. 180-95.
Everett, Barbara. *Auden*. Writers and Critics. Edinburgh: Oliver and Boyd, 1964.
Favichild, Hoxie Neale. *Religious Trends in English Poetry*. Vol. 11. New York: Columbia University Press, 1968.
Fitzgerald, David. "Auden's City." *The Dublin Magazine*, 6, no. 2 (1967), pp. 3-

17.
Fletcher, John Gould. "Poet of Courage." *Poetry*, 42 (May 1933), pp. 110-13.
Flint, F. Cudworth. "New Leaders in English Poetry." *Virginia Quarterly Review*, 14 (Autumn 1938), pp. 502-18.
Forster, E.M. *Two Cheers for Democracy*. New York: Harcourt, Brace, 1951.
Foxall, Edgar. "The Politics of W.H. Auden." *Bookman* (London), 85 (March 1934), pp. 474-75.
Fraser, G.S. *Vision and Rhetoric*. New York: Barnes and Noble, 1960.
Fremantle, Anne. "Wise Man's Sons." *Commonweal*, 41 (8 December 1944), pp. 194-98.
------. "Auden's Odyssey." *Commonweal*, 42 (25 May 1945), pp. 141-43.
Fuller, John. *A Reader's Guide to W.H. Auden*. London: Thames and Hudson, 1970.
------. "W.H. Auden's First Published Poems." *Notes and Queries*, 20 (September 1973), pp. 334-35.
Gersteuberger, Donna. "Poetry and Politics: The Verse Drama of Auden and Isherwood." *Modern Drama*, 5 (September 1962), pp. 123-32.
Gingerich, Martin. *W.H. Auden: A Reference Guide*. Boston: Mass: G.K. Hall, 1977.
Glicksberg, Charles I. "Poetry and Marxism: Three English Poets Take Their Stand." *University of Toledo Quarterly*, 6 (April 1937), pp. 309-25.
------. "Poetry and Social Revolution." *Dalhousie Review*, 17 (January 1938), pp. 493-503.
Gowda, H.H. Anniah. "W.H. Auden: A Tribute." *Literary Half-Yearly*, 15, No. 1 (1974), pp. 16-21.
Greenberg, Herbert. *Quest for the Necessary: W.H. Auden and the Dilemma of Divided Consciousness*. Cambridge: Harvard University Press, 1968.
Greenberg, Martin. "Auden as Critic." *Nation*, 170 (29 April), pp. 407-8.
Greenberg, Samuel. "W.H. Auden: Poet of Anxiety." *Masses and Mainstream*, 1 (June 1948), pp. 38-50.
Gregory, Horace. "The Liberal Critics and W.H. Auden." *New Masses*, 23 (20 April 1937), pp. 25-27.
------. "Of Vitality, Regionalism, and Satire in Recent American Poetry." *Sewanee Review*, 52 (Fall 1944), pp. 579-83.
Griffin, Howard. "The Idiom of W.H. Auden," *New Quarterly of Poetry*, 2 (Fall 1947), pp. 6-10.
------. "Conversation on Cornelia St.: A Dialogue with W.H. Auden." *Accent*, 10 (Autumn 1949), pp. 51-58.
Grigson, Geoffrey. "Notes on Contemporary Poetry," *Bookman* (London), 82 (September 1932), pp. 287-89.
------. "Auden as a Monster" *New Verse*, Nos. 26-27 (November 1937), pp. 13-17.
------. "Twenty-seven Sonnets." *New Verse*, 2 (May 1939), pp. 47-49.
Hamm, Victor M. "W.H. Auden: Pilgrim's Progress?" *America*, 73 (26 May

1945), pp. 156-57.
Hardy, Barbara. "Spears on Auden." *Essays in Criticism*, 15 (April 1965), pp. 230-38.
------. "W.H. Auden, Thirties to Sixties: A Face and a Map." *Southern Review*, 5 (Summer 1969), pp. 155-64.
Hausermann, H.W. "Left-Wing Poetry: A Note," *English Studies*, 21 (October 1939), pp. 203-13.
Haworth, Helen E. "Man's Tragic Dilemma in Auden and Sophocles." *Queen's Quarterly*, 77 (Winter 1970), pp. 566-76.
Hazard, Forrest E. "The Father Christmas Passage in Auden's 'Paid on Both Sides.'" *Modern Drama*, 12 (September 1969), pp. 155-64.
Henderson, Philip. "The Auden Age," *The Poet and Society*. London: Seeker and Warburg (1939), pp. 202-15.
Hoffman, Daniel G. *Paul Bunyan: Last of the Frontier Demigods*. Philadelphia: University of Pennsylvania Press (1952), pp. 143-53.
Hoggart, Richard. *Auden: An Introductory Essay*. New Haven: Yale University Press, 1951.
------. *W.H. Auden*. Writers and Their Work, No. 93. London: Longmans, 1957.
Hollander, John. "Auden at Sixty." *Atlantic*, 220 (July 1967), pp. 84-87.
Humphreys, A.R. "The Ascent of F6." *Cambridge Review*, 58 (30 April), pp. 353-55.
Hynes, Samuel. *The Auden Generation*. London: The Bodley Head, 1976.
------. "The Voice of Exile: Auden in 1940." *Sewanee Review*, 90 (Winter 1982), pp. 31-52.
Isherwood, Christopher. "Some Notes on Auden's Poetry." *New Verse*, Nos. 26-27 (November 1937), pp. 4-9.
------. *Lions and Shadows*. Norfolk, Connecticut: New Directions, 1947.
Iyengar, K.R. Srinivasa. "Mr. W.H. Auden (The King's Poetry Medalist)." *Journal of the University of Bombay*, 6 (May 1938), pp. 1-11.
Izzo, Carlo. "Goodbye to the Mezzogiorno." *Shenandoah*, 18 (Winter 1967), pp. 80-82.
Jameson, Storm. "W.H. Auden, the Poet of *Angst*." *Gate* (Oxford), 1 (December 1947), pp. 2-9.
Jarrell, Randall. "Changes of Attitude and Rhetoric in Auden's Poetry." *Southern Review*, 7 (1941), pp. 326-49.
------. "From Freud to Paul: The Stages of Auden's Ideology." *Partisan Review*, 12 (Fall 1945), pp. 437-57.
------. "Verse Chronicle." *The Nation*, 165 (18 October 1947), pp. 424-25.
------. "The Double Man." *Nation*, 152 (12 April 1941), pp. 440-41.
Jennings, Humphrey. "Eliot and Auden and Shakespeare." *New Verse*, 18 (December 1935), pp. 4-7.
Johnson, Richard A. *Man's Place: An Essay on Auden*. New York: Cornell University Press, 1973.

Johnson, Wendell Stacy. "Auden, Hopkins and the Poetry of Reticence." *Twentieth-Century Literature*, 20 (July 1974), pp. 165-71.

Jurak, Mirko. "English Political Verse Drama of the Thirties: Revision and Alteration." *Acta Neophilologica* (Ljvbljana), 1 (1968), pp. 67-78.

------. "The Group Theatre: Its Development and Significance for the Modern English Theatre." *Acta Neophilologica*, 2 (1969), pp. 3-43.

------. "Dramaturgic Concepts in the English Group Theatre: The Totality of Artistic Involvement." *Modern Drama*, 16 (June 1973), pp. 81-86.

Kallman, Chester. "Looking and Thinking Back." *London Magazine*, 6 (January 1967), pp. 80-82.

Kavanagh, Patrick. "Auden and the Creative Mind." *Envoy*, 5 (June 1951), pp. 33-39.

Kennedy, R.C. "The Classical Stance: W.H. Auden's Poetry." *Art International*, 16 (20 January 1972), pp. 60-65.

Kerman, Joseph. "Auden's 'Magic Flute'." *Hudson Review*, 10 (Summer 1957), pp. 309-16.

Kermode, Frank. "The Theme of Auden's Poetry: I." *Revista di Letterature Moderne Comparate*, 3 (March-June 1948), pp. 1-14.

------. "The Poet in Praise of Limestone." *Atlantic*, 225 (May 1970), pp. 67-71.

Larkin, Philip. "What's Become of Wystan?" *Spectator* (15 July 1960), pp. 104-5.

Leavis, F.R. "Mr. Auden's Talent." *Scrutiny*, 5 (December 1936), pp. 323-27.

------. *New Bearings in English Poetry*. Ann Arbor: University of Michigan Press, 1960.

Leehlitner, Ruth. "The Odyssey of Auden." *Poetry*, 66 (July 1945), pp. 204-15.

Lehmann, John. *New Writings in England*. New York: Critics Group Press, 1939.

------. *New Writing in Europe*. Harmondsworth: Penguin, 1940.

------. *The Whispering Gallery*. London: Longmans, Green, 1954.

Leinhardt, R.G. *The Importance of Scrutiny*, ed. Eric Bentley, New York: G.W. Stewart, 1948.

Marken, Ronald. "Power and Conflict in 'The Ascent of F6.'" *Discourse*, 7 (Summer 1964), pp. 277-82.

Mason, H.A. "Mr. Auden's Quartet." *Scrutiny*, 15 (Spring 1948), pp. 155-60.

Maxwell, D.E.S. "W.H. Auden: The Island and the City," *Poets of the Thirties*. London: Routledge and Kegan Paul, 1969.

McCoard, William, B. "An Interpretation of the Times: A Report on the Oral Interpretation of W.H. Auden's 'Age of Anxiety.'" *Quarterly Journal of Speech*, 35 (December 1949), pp. 489-95.

McDiarmid, Lucy S. "Auden and the Redeemed City: Three Allusions." *Criticism*, 13 (Fall 1971), pp. 340-50.

------, and John McDiarmid. "Artifice and Self-Consciousness in Auden's *The Sea and the Mirror*." *Contemporary Literature*, 16 (Summer 1975), pp. 353-77.

McDowell, Frederick P. *Aspects of American Poetry*. Ed. Richard M. Ludwig. Columbus: Ohio State University Press, 1962.

------. "Subtle, Various, Ornamental, Clever: Auden in His Recent Poetry." *Wisconsin Studies in Contemporary Literature*, 3 (Fall 1962), pp. 29-44.

MacNeice, Louis. "Letter to W.H. Auden." *New Verse*, Nos. 26-27 (November 1937), pp. 13-17.

------. *Modern Poetry*. New York: Oxford Press, 1938.

Mendelson, Edward. "The Coherence of Auden's *The Orators*." *English Literary History*, 35 (1968), pp. 114-33.

------. *Early Auden*. London: Faber, 1981.

Mitchell, Breon. "W.H. Auden and Christopher Isherwood: The 'German Influence'" *Oxford German Studies*, 1 (1966), pp. 163-72.

Mizner, Arthur. "Ideas in Auden," *Ascent Anthology*. New York: Harcourt, Brace, 1946.

Moore, Geoffrey. "Three Who Did Not Make a Revolution." *American Mercury*, 74 (April 1952), pp. 107-14.

Moore, Marianne. "W.H. Auden," *Predilections*. New York: Viking Press, 1954.

Morrison, Charles C. "The Faith of W.H. Auden," *The Christian Century*, 63 (16 January 1946), pp. 71-73.

Morse, Donald E. "The Nature of Man in Auden's 'For the Time Being.'" *Renascence*. 19 (Winter 1967), pp. 93-100.

--------. "'For the Time Being'": Man's Response to the Incarnation " Renascence, 19 (Summer 1967), pp. 190-97.

------. "Meaning of Time in Auden's *For the Time Being*." *Renascence*, 22 (Spring 1970), pp. 162-68.

Muir, Edwin. "Recent Poetry." *Purpose*, 12 (July-December 1940), pp. 149-52.

Nelson, Gerald. *Changes of Heart: A Study of the Poetry of W.H. Auden*. Perspectives in Criticism, No. 21. Berkeley: California University Press, 1968.

Newman, Michael. "The Art of Poetry." *Paris Review*, 14 (Spring 1974), pp. 32-69.

Norton, Dan S. "Auden's Poetry." *Virginia Quarterly Review*, 21 (Summer 1945), pp. 434-41.

Orwell, George. *Inside the Whale*. London: Gollancz, 1940.

Paulin, Tom. "In Search of Auden." *Sewanee Review*, 90 (Winter 1982), pp. 73-79.

Porteus, Hugh Gordon. "W.H. Auden." *Twentieth Century*, 4 (February 1933), pp. 14-16.

Powell, Dilys. *Descent from Parnassus*. London: The Cresset Press, 1934.

Pritchard, William H. *Seeing Through Everything*. London: Oxford University Press, 1977.

Replogle, Justin. "Social Philosophy in Auden's Early Poetry." *Criticism*, 2 (Fall 1960), pp. 351-61.

------. "The Gang Myth in Auden's Early Poetry." *Journal of English and*

Germanic Philosophy, 61, No. 3 (1962), pp. 481-95.

------. "Auden's Intellectual Development 1950-1960." *Criticism*, 7 (Summer 1965), pp. 250-62.

------. "Auden's Marxism." *PMLA*, 80 (December 1965), pp. 584-95.

------. "Auden's Religious Leap." *Wisconsin Studies in Contemporary Literature*, 7 (Winter-Spring 1966), pp. 47-75.

------. *Auden's Poetry*. Seattle: University of Washington Press, 1969.

Rickword, Edgell. "Auden and Politics." *New Verse*, Nos. 26-27 (November 1937), pp. 21-22.

Robinson, J.W. "W.H. Auden: Select Bibliography," *British Writers and Their Work*. No. 5. Lincoln, Nebraska: University of Nebraska, 1965.

Rosenthal, M.L. *The Modern Poets*. New York: Oxford University Press, 1960.

Roth, Robert. "The Sophistication of W.H. Auden: A Sketch in Longinian Method." *Modern Philology*, 48 (February 1951), pp. 193-204.

Savage, D.S. *The Personal Principle*. London: Routledge, 1944.

Savage, Henry. "Auden as Moralist." *Poetry Review*, 43 (January-February 1952), pp. 24-29.

Scarfe, Francis. *Auden and After: The Liberation of Poetry*, 1930-1941. London: Routledge, 1942.

Schwartz, Delmore. "The Two Audens." *Kenyon Review*, 1 (Winter 1939), pp. 34-45.

Scott, Nathan A. "The Poetry of W.H. Auden." *Chicago Review*, 22 (Winter 1959), pp. 53-75.

Seif, Morton. "The Impact of T.S. Eliot on Auden and Spender." *South Atlantic Quarterly*, 53 (January 1954), pp. 61-69.

Shepherd, T.B. "'For the Time Being': W.H. Auden's Christmas Oratorio." *London Quarterly and Holborn Review*, 177 (October 1952), pp. 277-84.

Sitwell, Edith. *Aspects of Modern Poetry*. London: Duckworth, 1934.

Smith, A.J.M. "Old Game, New Rules." *Poetry*, 47 (October 1935), pp. 43-46.

Southworth, James G. "Wystan Hugh Auden." *Sewanee Review*, 46 (April-June 1938), pp. 189-205.

Sparrow, John. *Sense and Poetry*. London: Constable, 1934.

Spears, Monroe K. "The Dominant Symbols of Auden's Poetry." *Sewanee Review*, 59 (July-September 1951), pp. 392-425.

------. "Late Auden: The Satirist as Lunatic Clergyman." *Sewanee Review*, 59 (January-March 1951), pp. 50-74.

------. "Auden in the Fifties: Rites of Homage." *Sewanee Review*, 69 (Summer 1961), pp. 375-98.

------. *The Poetry of W.H. Auden: The Disenchanted Island*. New York: Oxford University Press, 1963.

------. "Auden and Dionysus." *Shenandoah*, 18 (Winter 1967), pp. 85-95.

------. *Modern Poetry: Essays in Criticism*. Ed. John Hollander. New York: Oxford University Press, 1968.

------. *Dionysus and the City*. New York: Oxford University Press, 1970.

------. "In Memoriam W.H. Auden." *Sewanee Review*, 82 (Fall 1974), pp. 672-81.
------. "The Divine Comedy of W.H. Auden." *Sewanee Review*, 90 (Winter 1982), pp. 53-72.
Spender, Stephen. "Five Notes on W.H. Auden's Writing." *Twentieth Century*, 3 (July 1932), pp. 13-15.
------. *The Destructive Element: A Study of Modern Writers and Belief*. London: Jonathan Cape, 1935.
------. "Oxford to Communism." *New Verse*, Nos. 26-27 (November 1977), pp. 9-10.
------. "The Poetic Dramas of W.H. Auden and Christopher Isherwood." *New Writing*, 1 (Autumn 1938), pp. 24-25.
------. "The Importance of W.H. Auden." *London Mercury*, 39 (April 1939), pp. 613-18.
------. *Poetry Since 1939*. London: Longmans, Green, 1946.
------. "The Life of Literature." *Partisan Review*, 15 (1948), pp. 1311-31.
------. "W.H. Auden (1907-1973)." *Partisan Review*, 40, No. 3, pp. 546-48.
------, et. al. "W.H. Auden (1907-1973). *New Statesman*, 86 (5 October), pp. 478-80.
------,ed. *W.H. Auden: A Tribute*. New York: Macmillan, 1975.
------. *The Thirties and After: Poetry, Politics, People 1933-1970*. New York: Random House, 1978.
Srivatsava, Narasingh. *W.H. Auden, the Poet of Ideas*. New Delhi: S. Chand, 1978.
Staffer, Donald A. "Which Side Am I Supposed to Be On?" *Virginia Quarterly Review*, 22 (Autumn 1946), pp. 570-80.
Stanley, F.R. "Today the Struggle: A Critical Commentary on Auden's Sonnet-sequence *In Time of War*." *Literary Half-Yearly*, 6 (January 1965), pp. 74-88.
Stead, C.K. "Auden's 'Spain.'" *London Magazine*, N.S. 7 (March 1968), pp. 41-54.
Steinberg, Edwin R. "Poetic Drama in General and Auden and Isherwood in Particular." *Carnegie Studies in English*, 2 (1955), pp. 43-58.
Symons, Julian. "Auden and Poetic Drama 1938." *Life and Letters Today*, 20 (February 1939), pp. 70-79.
------. *The Thirties: A Dream Revolved*. London: The Cresset Press, 1960.
Tate, Allen. *Reason in Madness*. New York: Putnam, 1941.
Thurley, Geoffrey. *The Ironic Harvest*. New York: St. Martin's Press, 1974.
Thwaite, Anthony. "W.H. Auden: 1907-1973." *Literary Half-Yearly*, 15, No. 1 (1974), pp. 1-11.
Tolley, A.T. "The Thirties Poets at Oxford." *University of Toronto Quarterly*, 37 (July 1968), pp. 338-58.
Traversi, D.A. "Marxism and English Poetry" *Arena*, 1 (October-November 1937), pp. 199-211.

Turnell, G.M. "Two Notes on Modern English Poetry: I. Hopkins to W.H. Auden." *Colosseum*, 3 (June 1936), pp. 120-25.

Valgemae, Mardi. "Auden's Collaboration with Isherwood on *The Dog Beneath the Skin*." *Huntington Library Quarterly*, 31 (August 1968), pp. 373-83.

Waidson, H.M. "Auden and German Literature." *The Modern Language Review*, 70 (April 1975), pp. 347-65.

Walsh, William. "The Untransfigured Scene: The Personal Voice in Auden's Early Poetry." *Studies in the Twentieth Century*, 8 (Fall 1971), pp. 1-36.

Warren, Austin. "The Quest for Auden." *Sewanee Review*, 87 (Spring 1979), pp. 229-48.

Wasson, S. Carson. "A Descant on W.H. Auden's Christmas Oratorio." *Crozer Quarterly*, 23 (October 1946), pp. 340-49.

Weales, Gerald. "A Little Faith, a Little Envy: A Note on Santayana and Auden." *American Scholar*, 24 (Summer 1955), pp. 340-47.

Weatherhead, A. Kingsley. "British Leftist Poetry of the Nineteen Thirties." *Michigan Quarterly Review*, 10 (Winter 1971), pp. 12-22.

Weisstein, Ulrich. "Reflections on a Golden Style: W.H. Auden's Theory of Opera." *Comparative Literature*, 22 (Spring 1970), pp. 108-24.

Whittermore, Reed. "Auden on Americans." *Sewanee Review*, 65 (Winter 1957), pp. 145-51.

Williams, Raymond. *Drama from Ibsen to Eliot*. London: Chatto and Windus, 1952.

Wilson, Edmund. "The Oxford Boys Becalmed," *The Shores of Light*. New York: Farrar, Strauss, 1952.

------. "W.H. Auden in America." *New Statesman and Nation*, 51 (9 June 1956), pp. 658-59.

Wright, George T. *W.H. Auden*. Twayne United States Authors Series, 144. New York: Twayne, 1969.

Index